HOW THE WEATHER REALLY WORKS!

Peter Bros

1994

PUBLISHED BY FINANCIAL BOOK PARTNERS

PRINTED IN THE UNITED STATES OF AMERICA

ISBN 0-9627769-4-7

Designed by Lemieux Creative Enterprises

HOW THE WEATHER **REALLY** WORKS!

PETER BROS

FBP BOOKS TELL YOU ABOUT YOURSELF AND THE
WORLD YOU OCCUPY

COPERNICAN SERIES

VOLUME 2

The Cooling Continuum: The Rise and Fall of Species
on Earth

VOLUME 3

Atoms, Stars and Minds: Synthesizing an Elementary
Particle That Comprehends Itself

RELATED TITLES

The Model Mind: How the Mind Moves Matter

How The Weather Really Works!

1   What the Weather Isn't

Fortunately, for most of my life, I have been able to ignore the weather.

I lived for seven years in Greensboro, North Carolina, where the only weather I remember was an early morning ice storm. The only reason that I remember it was because I couldn't walk on the sidewalk without slipping and falling. I was maybe four or five at the time, and it remained nothing more than an interesting memory.

Because I had always heard that the weather was impossible to predict, let alone explain, especially in Washington, D.C., where I have lived since 1947, I was glad that I could ignore it, happy that it was not an operative factor in my life.

And yet, the weather is always there, humming in the background of our consciousness, dictating what we wear, where we can go and what we can do once we get there.

Weather is never far away!

When I was in my early teens, I got into a little disagreement with three or four family members and friends about the weather, or more specifically, about the wind. We were sitting in a kitchen in Maryland, and a storm was brewing from the northwest. Wind had started to pick up, and someone commented that the air pressure must be dropping at a rapid rate.

Why, I wondered, could that be concluded from the wind blowing.

After some discussion, I was told that the air pressure represents the weight of the air, and that when there is air with high pressure next to air with low pressure, the air seeks to equalize the difference in air pressure. The process of equalization results in the wind as the air moves from the high pressure area to the low pressure area.

This, although sounding reasonably sensible to me, wasn't the way I was visualizing what was happening.

Having attempted in my earliest memories to position myself with respect to the world in which I existed, both as to space and as to time, I had built up a picture of myself sitting on the face of the Earth, at just under the fortieth parallel (we were in the middle of the Korean Police Action and parallel was being used for latitude), moving at a rate of just under eight hundred miles per hour in a easterly direction.

Now, just like the Declaration of Independence, I held this fact to be self-evident: If I moved north, my rate of motion would decrease, and if I moved south, my rate of motion would increase.

Not only did I take this fact to be self-evident, I assumed that everyone else took it the same way, and that it could be assumed in discussion.

Thus, when the discussion concluded with the decision that the wind was blowing because it was moving from a high pressure area to a low pressure area, I pointed out that it seemed more logical to me that the air that was moving up from the south was slowing down to match the speed of the Earth's surface, but was none the less moving faster than the air to the north. The result, I ventured, was to create a sort of vacuum along the separation between the two air masses which caused the air from the north to speed up.

What, I was asked, did I mean when I said that air was slowing down. Air was clearly speeding up because the wind was blowing. We know what is happening, we are just trying to explain to you why.

I answered that the air that we were standing in was moving at about eight hundred miles an hour, as were we, and that...

That was enough of that foolishness. The air outside the window didn't move unless the wind was blowing. When the wind was blowing, then we could discuss what made the wind blow. Otherwise, go play!

It wasn't the time to bring up the fact that we were not only moving at eight hundred miles an hour in a circle with a point on the Earth's axis as a center, but that we were traveling at a pretty good clip in a circle around the sun, and, to add dizzying dimensions to the situation, we were traveling really fast in the arm of the galaxy of which the sun was a part.

I hadn't mentioned the last two motions because they had no apparent effect on the weather, at least the day to day weather that we seek to explain.

But then, not only was the first motion not acknowledged, its existence was vehemently denied!

If this motion wasn't being taken into consideration by the people trying to figure out the weather, it would be a major factor in not being able explain the weather.

It seemed at the time that failing to take this motion into consideration would produce some pretty incomplete pictures of what was happening with weather. After all, the moisture that produces much of the weather is supposedly being evaporated at the equator, and thus into air masses that are moving at a thousand miles an hour. These air masses, because of the temperature differentials between the equator and the poles, differentials which produce heavier cold air masses that move in gradients toward the equator, move north.

As they move north, these air masses have to slow down to match the progressively slower movement of the surface of the planet beneath them!

I was in the seventh grade at the time, and while it was not the first time that my view of physical reality had been negated by consensus, I still had an abiding, albeit fuzzy faith that education was like trade unions or secret societies in that you had to learn at one level before you could hope to understand at the next level.

It did give me pause, however.

My views about physical reality had been negated in

other areas that I thought were quite important to understanding the weather. Electricity, which Ben Franklin demonstrated lightning to be, was something that was measurable rather than understandable. Every time I pierced the mumbo jumbo of terms and symbols, I always came up with nothing that was objective. Everything was defined in terms of everything else, and nothing came right out and said what electricity was.

What was happening when different materials set up a difference in potential, and how did it relate to doing the same thing with spinning magnetic fields?

No one was interested in talking about it. If we could measure it, it was, and that was enough.

Lightning, too, was off bounds. I had early decided that what gives off light burns, and thus light must be made up of what was burning.

Because electric companies bill you on the amount of electricity you use up, I figured that the electricity was being converted into light by the filament of a light bulb.

Lightning, then, was simply the direct conversion of electricity to light.

Unfortunately, I quickly learned that what produces light doesn't go into making up light, and what causes electricity isn't going into making up light either.

Questioning what gravity was, of course, was a form of insanity.

The attractive force holds the atmosphere to the Earth,

and thus is what generates the force that causes the atmosphere to move at the same rate as the surface of the Earth moves.

But more to the point, gravity is what causes the same air masses to exert more pressure or less pressure depending on the conditions of the air mass.

It seemed to me to be important to understand how gravity worked in order to understand how it affected air masses.

However, I quickly learned that gravity wasn't available to be understood, it was available to be accepted as an irrefutable and unquestionable fact, and that was that.

I also learned that an Earth that sprouted volcanoes in the most unseemly places, volcanoes that spewed forth smoke and fire from the bowels of the Earth didn't really represent the Earth.

The question was interesting, because if I wanted to understand how temperature affects air masses, and thus air mass pressure, I would have to know where the temperature was coming from.

Imagine my surprise, then, when I found out that the Earth produced no temperature contribution to atmospheric temperature, but that incoming radiation scientifically balanced outgoing radiation. All of the atmosphere's temperature came from the sun, and that was that. Volcanoes are something entirely different, unless, of course, they produce enough ash to blot out the sun.

So you see, my ability to ignore the weather was really the result of my total ignorance of the conditions that went into making the weather.

I was even wrong when it came to the atom!

One of the most interesting aspects about the weather was the water that seemed to drive it.

Water had the ability to appear in three forms, as water itself, in the oceans and lakes, surfaces available to contribute the water in its second, or vapor form to the atmosphere.

Once the water was in the atmosphere, it changed the very nature of that atmosphere, and could end up in its third form, ice.

This stuff was amazing, at least in my viewpoint. What in the world is happening when the same molecules can appear as a liquid, a gas and a solid.

Melting ice takes heat out of the environment while freezing water puts heat into the environment.

What in the world was heat?

The atom available to explain all of these marvels was static. It had a fixed number of charged particles which accounted for its ability to chemically interact. To balance that charge, it had an identical number of oppositely charged particles in the nucleus. To account for weight, it had another particle, with heavier atoms having more of these particles than lighter atoms.

The atom didn't seem to have the capability of explaining heat, light, the ability of ice to soak up heat as it melted and water to give it off as it froze or the ability of air masses to gain weight when they lost water and lose weight when they gained water.

The atom we had to live with seemed to have been constructed by people who, like me, were totally ignorant of the weather.

At the time, I couldn't argue about atoms, gravity, the unity of light and electricity, or the contribution of the Earth's internal heat to it surface environment. I was at the bottom of the learning pile. I had no ammunition. As a result, I had to rely on a belief that, as I went along, all of these things, with their incomprehensible explanations, would sort themselves out.

But the discussion on the northwest wind impressed me because there was nothing that required sorting out. I may have doubted my reservations about the official explanation for, say, electricity, but I damn well knew that the air outside the window was traveling at about eight hundred miles an hour, just as I was traveling at eight hundred miles an hour!

I knew that the air was newly arrived from the equator, where it had been going about a thousand miles an hour.

I therefore knew that the air was slowing down, even though it appeared to be speeding up!

This is an inarguable fact.

But I couldn't argue the fact because, as I learned later when I attempted to re-open the discussion, facts are what reality appears to be rather than what reality is!

I left weather in search of answers to all of those other questions, questions about how gravity works, how electricity works, how atoms are constituted, what heat is and how it moves, and even the question raised by the last paragraph, the question of why we see what we recall rather than the reality that exists.

We live in the modern world, protected by the scientific method and rational discourse, with open access to a community that is willing to test all hypotheses. Wouldn't the simple fact that air has to slow down as it moves north be the basis of a factual discussion, or at least the basis for a discussion?

Just try it!

Don't try mass/gravity, either, unless you want to end up on the funny farm. Fortunately, in discussing how the weather really works, we only have to mention in passing how the attractive force operates, and only then because the principal that drives the mechanism that causes attraction, induction, provides the raw material that drives the weather.

The weather is explainable, but not by current concepts. Specifically, current concepts of electricity, combustion, heat, light and the atom are not adequate.

The concepts that can be used to explain the weather are concepts derived to explain, rather than define, electricity, combustion, heat, light and the atom as applied to the movement of matter, the Earth and the atmosphere in physical reality.

How the weather really works is understandable, but to understand, you will have to drop just about every mental crutch you have been given to support your reality.

Wind doesn't blow because it is moving from high pressure areas to low pressure areas. The jet stream does not drop down from the north, dragging cold weather behind it. Nothing turns right because of the Coriolis effect. Particles of air don't conserve motion in momentum!

Rather, weather is the various storm systems that organize themselves as a result of the lower, dry, southward moving air masses lagging the Earth's rotation under the upper, ice flecked, northward moving air masses outracing that same rotation.

Weather does not result from water evaporating into warm air at the equator and wafting north on tropical currents.

Rather, the key to weather is determining how the moving air masses transport heat in the environment.

Water molecules do not vaporize and freeze.

Rather, the atoms that make up water molecules breakdown and recombine as the air masses that move them alter their position within the environment.

Weather is not what you think it is.

Rather, it is everything you've never thought it was!

What I am going to do in this short book is attempt to familiarize you with the basic physical principals that underlie the weather.

These physical principals are going to contradict what you might have learned in chemistry, physics and electricity 101.

But they are the principles that make up the physical reality of the world in which we exist, and the fact that so many of them come together to explain how weather really works is a tribute to the complex nature of weather, and its ability to defy rational discourse.

My interest is that they do come together to explain a field for which there is no clear explanation.

Concepts, such as the atom, the electron, the photon and heat are not subject to proof by the scientific method.

The atom, for instance, is designed to explain physical phenomena. Making physical representations concerning concepts of how the atom explains physical phenomena, making pretty pictures of the atom or graphically incorporating the atom into movies does not make the atom any more real.

The atom is merely a concept!

The notion that we can devise a methodology that can

prove concepts is as erroneous as the idea that facts have to be proven.

The existence of facts merely has to be demonstrated, and the scientific method does this admirably as long as the facts are directly measurable.

When facts are not directly measurable, they are not facts, and no man made procedure can turn them into facts.

The scientific method cannot make concepts facts. As a result, the only factual basis for our concept of an atom is the atom's ability to explain facts.

I have constructed an atom to explain how matter formed, how it produced physical matter, how that physical matter could produce chemical matter, how the physical matter and the chemical matter could produce electricity and light, and how that light in turn could effect physical matter.

The atom, as luck would have it, also explains how water can turn into ice, and clouds can turn into water, talking in or giving up heat in the process.

Having an atom that provides a physical description of how hydrogen and oxygen can interact so that they add heat to and remove heat from the environment as the environmental temperature changes goes a long way in explaining the weather.

Thus, in order for you to understand how the weather really works, you will have to understand how this atom is constructed, and how it works in physical reality.

Many of your other concepts will also be affected.

Electricity as a moving charge doesn't really describe anything, although the inductances electricity creates, we will find, are all pervasive.

Nor will the idea that there is polarity connected to electricity serve a useful purpose. This little mis-step in the effort to come up with a consistent picture of physical phenomena kind of snuck into the thought processes because electricity was produced by and affected physical magnets. It's an example of applying conclusions about something we know nothing about, magnetism, to something else we know nothing about, electricity so that we can define two things that we know nothing about with the same terms.

If you have had the problem, as I had, of trying to figure out how there can be a positive and negative point in a perfectly symmetrical circuit, you will be relieved to find out that electricity, like light, has as a property, movement, and once you have movement, you merely need direction, something that can be provided without polarity.

Because light and electricity both have the property of movement, and it is well established that one is convertible into the other, we can abandon the concept that the two are different.

But that will all become clear as we go along.

And I hasten to add, what do we really know when we know that gravity is a property of mass, electricity is a moving charge or magnetism is the result of the alignment of molecular magnets?

Nothing!

At the end of the book, you will not only be able to explain the weather, you will be able to explain these, and other physical phenomena.

Not only will you have to change preconceived notions, assumptions which you are probably not aware you have, you are going to have to adopt new concepts.

The major example of this is the concept of presence.

Presence is really a simple concept. It involves visualizing a string of elementary particles moving at the speed of light right in front of your eyes. At any point in the stream, there is an elementary particle.

How can this be?

Simply because at any point in the stream, as one particle leaves the point another particle enters the point.

At any point in a flow of elementary particles, there is always a particle present!

Why is presence important?

Because it explains field replacement, another new concept.

If you take the current picture of an atom, with a

negative electron orbiting a positive proton, and do away with the concept of magnets derived from playing with kissing dogs, that opposites attract, you can substitute the concept that the electron moves toward a potential difference created by a deficit of electrons.

With this concept you can picture the orbiting electron's motion being held in a circular orbit by its tendency to move toward a potential difference created by a deficit of electrons in the nucleus. The potential difference of the nucleus isn't enough to overcome the forward motion of the electron, but it is enough to hold it in orbit, in much the same way that we think of gravity holding the God given motion of the planets in orbit.

With that picture in mind, we can analyze what would happen to the orbiting electron if a flow of electrons passed the nucleus of the atom.

Because the flow has presence, with an electron at each point in the flow as long as the flow exists, then the presence of the flow is stationary with respect to the nucleus.

Because the presence of the flow satisfies the potential difference caused by a deficit of electrons in the nucleus, there is no reason for the orbiting electron to stay in orbit, and it can fly off in search of another potential difference.

Remove the flow, and the potential difference of the nucleus reasserts itself, and the nucleus captures an electron wherever it can.

The field is the flow, the replacement is the field replacing the need of the nucleus for orbiting elementary particles.

Now all you have to do is forget the idea that the atom has a fixed number of electrons and that they orbit at specific levels in specific numbers, and your mind will be free to picture the atom with a cloud of orbiting electrons, billions of the things, and flows of electrons, manmade electricity or light, or simply sunlight as flows of electrons that, by their presence, replace the need of the atom for orbiting electrons, which fly off into space as long as the field is present, but which are attracted back when the field is removed, and you have a pretty good picture of what's happening, whether it be electricity, combustion, or crystallization.

The concepts of non polarity, presence and field replacement are not hard to grasp. When we see them working to make up the reality in which we exist, they will come clear.

What is hard about new concepts is that they contradict what we have learned to be reality.

Like the wind blowing, we know that it is speeding up!

When we find that it is only slowing down less quickly, reality disagrees with the reality we really see, the reality we have learned to recall.

Because we understand reality by comparing it with our recall, we actually see with our recall, and when reality does not agree with our recall, we have a tendency to distrust reality!

Most of the problem with the current picture, or more appropriately, lack of a picture, of the weather is the silly notion that the Earth is spinning in frictionless space.

Newton's idea of planetary motion in frictionless space is a dog that won't die. It's long been known that space is full of activity, but the idea that the planet is spinning as a result of some past force should never have been born.

Laplace retrofitted Newton's failure to explain motion with a historical force to explain rotation, but the analysis of the weather, of all physical phenomena, should have disclosed that without a force to maintain the Earth's rotation, the weather is unexplainable.

Instead, in an ill conceived attempt at scientific legitimacy, explanations of the weather have insisted on adopting God as an explanation for the Earth's rotation, and in the process, made weather unexplainable.

Readers interested in what makes the Earth rotate can read Chapter Twelve, The Movement of Matter in Space: Rotation, in <u>Atoms, Stars and Minds: Synthesizing an Elementary Particle That Comprehends Itself</u>.

Readers that wish to continue living the fantasy that weather organizes itself in a way that won't affect the frictionless rotation of the Earth in space can read something else!

I plan to make this book as simple as possible.

I normally run a parallel text in boxes in an attempt to have a second chance at explaining, but we are not talking about planetary rotation, the operation of the mind or the origin of life.

We are talking about weather, so I think that a straight forward text will suffice.

I will also resist the use of drawings. I don't do it well, and I can't get anyone else to do it for me. However, everybody draws to their own understanding, so it wouldn't hurt for you to draw a bit as you go along. I have left ample room in the margins and it always seems to make things a little clearer.

Once in a while I will refer to a fact, say the attraction of conductors by their inductances or the seasonal movement of the sun's ecliptic plane, without immediate explanation.

Although all explanations can't be made at once, all explanations will be made.

Finally, I don't expect this to be a long drawn out book. I will attempt to craft chapters somewhere in the four thousand word range, and I can't see more than ten chapters.

Actually, I'm looking at this as a sort of fun book as well as an educational experience for me, exploring the obvious with the not so obvious.

I hope it's the same for you!

2   The Electron: The Universal Elementary
       Particle

Matter is made up of molecules, which are atoms of various types of matter held together in a manner that the matter presents specific characteristics.

We are all familiar with water, which is considered to be a molecule that is made up of two hydrogen atoms and one oxygen atom.

The atom, and the various molecules that combinations of atoms create are conceptual structures born of the chemist's need to manipulate matter to specific purposes.

Concepts are only as good as the facts they explain. If the concept of the atom were perfect, then any type of matter could be predicted and created without further ado.

The fact is, much of the advancement on the chemical front is the result of patient trial and error, the classic use of the scientific method to sniff around facts in reality, get an idea about a reality that we don't know, and then try to create that reality. We learn as much from our failures as from our successes, and many of our successes are accidental, having nothing to do with the idea that led us in the direction that produced them.

When our experimentation has a solid footing in reality, the discovery of facts easily outpaces the conceptual underpinnings we use to explain the facts.

When experimentation has no solid footing in reality, false concepts about reality are not disproven. Instead of facts outpacing concepts, the opposite occurs. Concepts that remain disproven for long periods of time become facts!

In the process, they exclude consideration of other facts that cry out for explanation.

The further the concepts are from reality, the less chance they have of being disproven.

We end up with a pretty strange pile of concepts dictating our recall, and thus our reality.

This problem haunts almost every area of modern science, and specifically, the many areas that stand between ourselves and an understanding of how the weather really works.

The atom, however, having a solid footing in reality, is one of the most successful concepts in history. And I am speaking of the atom that is used in chemistry, rather than its chimerical progeny evolved by physicists!

Structurally, the current concept of the chemical atom has electrons orbiting a nucleus made up of neutrons and protons.

The neutrons and protons do not come into play in creating chemical interactions. Thus, the atom's success is based solely on the concept of an electron that can share orbits. By fixing the number of electrons in orbits in specific shells, shells which are designed to reflect the periodic table of elements which arranges matter by its physical characteristics, this atom has been successful in organizing knowledge about chemical interactions.

The addition of the neutron to account for weight was a sort of sliding bonus. It didn't affect the atom's ability to explain chemical interactions. Even though the only purpose of the atom was to explain chemical interactions, an atom that didn't explain weight was certainly not a complete atom.

An atom that explained chemical interaction without explaining the most obvious characteristic of matter, weight, was just not a salable atom.

Forget the fact that we haven't the foggiest idea what causes weight!

It's sufficient if an answer makes us think we know.

Like the neutron, the addition of the proton didn't affect the atom's ability to explain chemical interactions. But the proton is not necessary to satisfy an apparent characteristic of matter, such as weight.

What is the proton's purpose?

Certainly not to hold the atoms together into molecules. Protons were defined as charged particles. "Like" charges are supposed to repel.

This left the orbiting electrons to hold the atoms together into molecules.

How, I had wondered in chemistry class, did orbiting

electrons hold atoms together in molecules? They don't, conceptually, unless you consider atoms sheep and electrons sheep dogs!

I am going to deconstruct the atom and reconstruct it in a way that it doesn't have useless or unworkable knobs and dials.

To accomplish this, we can focus on the question of the proton's purpose.

The addition of the proton to the atom is an example of how unexamined concepts can sort of slide into our recall so that they dictate the reality that we see.

Why do we need a proton in the atom?

Because we believe that like charges repel and opposite charges attract! If the orbiting electron is being attracted to the nucleus, then the nucleus has to have an opposite charge!

Where does this limitation on our thinking come from?

What edict decrees that like charges repel?

Come to think of it, what is a charge, and how are opposite charges qualitatively different?

The answers are a lot simpler than the questions, but it takes questions to define the answers!

To understand where the proton came from, let's transfer the concept of electrons orbiting an atom from the atom to a crystalline structure whose atoms share orbiting electrons.

In order for contiguous atoms to share electrons, they have to orbit all of the atoms in the physical structure. To do this, the orbits have to be external to the crystalline structure itself.

This is a magnet!

In a magnet, electrons come in one end, pass through the material and exit the other end, only to orbit around the structure and re-enter the material at the first end.

Magnets are considered to generate magnetic lines of force that stretch out in bands defined by the ends of the magnet. Because no one knows what magnetic lines of force are, we can feel confident in defining them as external flows of electrons, electrons that orbit a physical structure rather than the individual nuclei of the atoms that make up the structure.

This would permit the definition of magnetic material to be a molecular structure that permits a portion of the atom's orbiting electrons to orbit the structure itself, and thus to establish external orbits. We could even test the reality of this by moving a conductor through these orbiting flows of electrons to see if we could knock some out into the conductor, thereby creating an electrical flow.

But that's done all over the world by electric utilities on a pretty constant basis, so there is nothing to test!

Realizing that if it is not testable, it cannot be a scientific fact, we'll just have to content ourselves with the knowledge that we are only dealing with facts.

Now, if you take an end of a magnet where the orbiting electrons are coming out, and place it against the end of another magnet where the electrons are going in, the electrons coming out of the one magnet will continue on into the other, and the orbiting electrons will force the magnets together, just like the inductances of conductors with electric flows moving in the same direction force the conductors to move together.

If you try to hold the two ends at which the flows are either entering or exiting together, then the magnets are pushed apart, either by the exiting flows, or by the external flows returning to enter the magnets.

From this factual situation, the mental construct of opposites attracting and likes repelling became ingrained in the mind, assumptions to the thought process. Because no one had figured out what was actually going on, the rote words became catechism, with the assumption becoming reality and attempts to think past the words discouraged by threats of excommunication.

Fortunately, because one end of a magnet always points north, and the opposite of north is south, this mental construct of opposites attracting and likes repelling can be scientifically proven on a repeated basis. All we have to do is let two magnets point north and then paint those ends. The painted ends will always attract the unpainted ends, and painted ends will always repel each other, as will the unpainted ends.

As we can see, by simply externalizing the orbits of

electrons which in all other matter is internalized, there is a physical reason why magnets attract and repel the way they do.

There is no mysterious force having two faces, a Janus of the unknown.

We simply have a physical reaction in reality!

Puzzling over magnets for several thousand years didn't disclose their secrets, however, and thus, like the proverbial elephant, never forgetting the concept of opposites, our search for universal truth next noted that rubbing a glass rod with a silk scarf resulted in a glass rod that would attract non magnetic matter such as bits of paper. The silk scarf, in turn, would get a case of static cling.

This was in the middle of several hundred years during which the Phlogiston Theory was used to explain combustion. Phlogiston was a sort of spiritual liquid that imbued matter and the medium that the matter occupied. When matter underwent combustion, it was thought to be giving off phlogiston.

It was during this period that Ben Franklin experimented with electrical effects. Being surrounded by the concept of phlogiston, Franklin thought that when the silk scarf rubbed the glass rod, liquid moved from the silk to the rod, giving the rod a positive charge, as opposed to the silk scarf, which was left with a negative charge.

Franklin thought in terms of charges because suddenly

discharging the silk would create a spark which he decided was the same spark found in lightning.

Here we had an unfortunate confluence of effects. The glass rod attracted paper like a magnet attracted another magnet, and the silk scarf gave off sparks.

Thus began the confusion between the north and south ends of the magnet with electricity. The magnet gave rise to the concept of opposites attracting and likes repelling, so that when we saw a glass rod attracting paper, we thought in terms of opposites attracting. We couldn't call the charges north and south because they resided in two separate objects, so we thought in terms of fluid moving from one object to the other object, leaving the object from which it moved with less liquid, a minus and the object to which it moved with more liquid, a plus.

The plus and minus were concepts that indicated that the amount of fluid in the scarf and the glass rod was not in balance with the amount of fluid that made up the environment, the surrounding air. This disbalance was the charge, with the glass rod being positively charged and the silk scarf holding a negative charge.

Keep in mind that the only reason that we had for carrying the concept that like charges repel into the realm of charges was the fact that the positively charged rod would attract bits of non magnetic paper.

Faraday came along and observed that there were actually external flows moving between the opposite poles of a magnet. This was after the death of the Phlogiston

Theory and he didn't know what was flowing. But then again, it wasn't clear what was moving between the silk scarf and the glass rod either.

Ignorance notwithstanding, however, Faraday could analogize the scarf to one end of the magnet and the glass rod to the other end of the magnet.

The magnetic poles, north and south, were unlike magnetic poles.

The scarf and rod, after the rubbing, one with a negative charge, the other with a positive charge, held unlike charges.

What could be more logical than to generalize that magnetic lines of force joined unlike magnetic poles or opposite electric charges!

He then concluded from the generalization that unlike poles or charges pulled poles or charges together while like poles or charges caused the poles or charges to repel each other.

And, lo and behold, the requirement that opposites attract and likes repel was rooted in any conceptualizations we might make about what was happening when we rubbed a glass rod with a silk scarf, and by extension, to any analysis of electrical phenomena.

Such are the rigorous processes used to legitimize the authority of modern, consensual science!

Later, when the electron was conceptualized to define electrical phenomena, it had to conform to concepts of likes and opposites. Thus, to move in a circuit, the electron had to move toward an opposite charge.

If the phlogistic concept of fluid moving from one element to another element had been left alone, we wouldn't need to have positive and negative charges to explain the flow of electrons.

We could simply have electrons moving from the silk to the glass, or in today's conceptualization of the process, moving from the glass to the silk. When we pad around the rug, we are picking up electrons which later jump to the doorknob if we don't ground ourselves first.

The current conceptualization of the situation has positive as the state that exists when there is an absence of electrons and negative as the state that exists when there is an excess of electrons.

Whatever the conceptualization, we don't need a positive and a negative charge to describe a flow of electrons. We only need a potential difference, a situation in which one group of atoms has a deficit of electrons when compared to another group of atoms. When the two groups of atoms are connected, electrons flow to the group of atoms with the deficit of electrons until both groups of atoms have the same potential difference with respect to their environment.

Now, the assumption that opposites attract creates the notion that it takes an opposite charge to set electrons in motion. As you move the white dog near the black dog, the black dog all of a sudden starts to move, and snaps its lips on the lips of the white dog.

This notion is that it is the principle that opposites attract that gives the electron its motion.

This notion of motion is a real slider, an unexamined assumption of the first order.

We will see that, by recognizing that motion is a property of the electron, all the electron needs is a place to which it can move.

That place is any place that has a deficit of electrons with respect to the electrons that, as a result of the deficit, become available to move.

There is no need for positive and negative charges, and there is certainly no need to transfer the concept, inaccurate even for magnets, that opposites attract and likes repel, to electricity.

And beyond!

But transfer we did, so that when a defined concept of an atom was moving into our consciousness, and we needed shell electrons to move back and forth between two atoms in order to explain chemical interactions, the question arose, what is keeping the shell electrons from flying off into space?

Worse yet, what's balancing the negative charge? After all, non charged matter must be the result of opposite charges balancing each other!

If the electrons are negative, then we need a positive

charge to balance the negative charge and hold the electrons in orbit. We added neutrons to explain weight. We'll just add positively charged protons to balance the electrons we need for chemical interactions.

I am not going to go into the damage physicists have wrought on this conceptualization of the classic atom with its defined electrons orbiting a nucleus composed of neutrons and protons. Suffice it to say that the rigorous application of the scientific method to the task of systematically converting concepts into facts has created an atom which can predict anything while explaining nothing!

The point I want to make is that we really don't need a positive charge in the nucleus. All we need is something to attract the negative charge, to keep it from flying off into space, while producing a non charged atom.

The idea that opposites attract is so ingrained in our thought processes that we cannot possibly see two electrons attracting each other.

But all the idea of opposites attracting does to us is make us conceptually blind to the obvious, that if you remove electrons from matter that is in balance with its environment, then it is going to attempt to attract the electrons back out of the environment!

Let's do another take on this because it is so important.

If we have a glass rod with no charge, which means that it is in balance with its environment, and we do something that will remove some of the electrons orbiting the atoms that make up the rod, then we have disbalanced the glass rod with respect to its environment. It will want to recapture electrons out of the environment so that it will once again be in balance.

It will attract a piece of paper simply because the paper has electrons and can move.

We don't need a proton to do the attracting. All we need is a bunch of electrons held together into a structure by their own potential difference with the environment.

Remove one electron from the structure and the potential difference of the structure increases, increasing the structure's ability to attract the electron back out of the environment.

If we are going to construct an atom out of electrons, and we are, we are going to have to create an electron with properties that result in all of the situations in which we measure electrons, including electrical flows, the chemical interaction of atoms and magnetism.

How could we go about finding out what these properties might be?

We have already seen one of the properties, motion. Electricity, like light, slows down when it enters a medium, and then speeds back up when it exits the medium.

The speed of electricity is measured by creating a spark at one end of a very long conductor, and then measuring the time it takes for a spark to be produced at the other end of the conductor.

Because our electron is going to be the same particle that makes up light, we can say that it is traveling at the speed of light when it is unimpaired by any other force.

When we induce a flow of electrons by creating a potential difference in a conductor, which is a difference between the presence of a source of electrons and a place where there is a deficit of electrons, then electrons will move to the deficit of electrons at a speed that is the speed of light less the resistance in the conductor.

This concept, that electrons are at rest when they are traveling at the speed of light, is very important. You can readily see that electrons that are bound into making up the atoms that make up matter have a tremendous potential for regaining their speed, and thus their energy if they are somehow released from being bound up in the atoms making up the matter.

I use motion as one of the two properties of the electron, the elementary particle that we are going to use to construct the atom, because motion is one of the two things that we know are occurring in reality.

Light moves from stars to the Earth. If it didn't, we couldn't see the stars.

If light is moving, then it is reasonable to assume that it is either being propelled to move, or it is moving because that is what it does when it is not doing anything.

Modern science sees light as being propelled by alternating collapsing electric and magnetic fields. We could disregard this explanation solely on the basis that modern science has no idea what electric or magnetic fields are, let alone how they might collapse.

However, a better reason to reject the propellant concept out of hand is modern science's absolute ignorance of the nature of light, which it medievally analogizes to, of all things, water waves!

But the real reason to disregard the propellant concept is that it has light traveling forever. However desirable it is to keep thousands of astronomers on the payroll, the simple fact of the matter is that light expands, and as it does so, it diminishes.

Something that diminishes eventually disappears, a fact that contradicts light generated by alternating collapsing electric and magnetic fields!

"At rest motion" is the concept that the electron moves in its normal state, and it is what we are going to use as one of the two properties of the electron.

I used light as an example because we are going to use the same elementary particle, the electron, to describe light. After all, motion, as a property of the electron, assumes energy because restraining the motion of the particle creates a potential for energy.

If motion is one thing that we know is happening in reality, what is the other thing that is happening in reality?

Whatever it is that restrains motion!

We know that matter has substance.

We know that whatever is making up the paper on which this book is printed is not traveling through space at the speed that the light we are reading it by is traveling.

The matter that makes up the page, and makes up all matter, is in fact, held together by something.

It may well be that some of the matter is orbiting electrons, electrons that are whizzing around nuclei at close to the speed of light, a speed diminished by the electrons need to orbit the nuclei. But as a whole, the matter that is making up the paper is stationary with respect to, say, the light bouncing off its surface.

If it is stationary, then something is holding it in place!

We have, for the past three hundred years, had this concept of mass. Mass is thought to be what matter is, and the attractive force, gravity, is said to be a property of the matter that is the mass.

If the fact that no one can find gravity in the matter that makes up the mass that produces it is any indication, gravity isn't holding anything together on an atomic level.

There is a perfectly good explanation of what produces the attractive force that we call gravity, and it doesn't involve the internal makeup of the atom, where it doesn't exist in any event.

However, we need an attractive force to hold the atom,

and thus matter, together, and the atom is where we want to locate the electron.

Let's look at what gravity is conceived to be so that we can create a property of attraction, the second property of the electron that holds matter together, that isn't anything like gravity!

One of the neat things about gravity is that, while it diminishes inversely with the square of its distance from the source, it is never used up. If the Earth's gravity has "X" effect on Jupiter when Jupiter is on the same side of the sun as the Earth, then when Jupiter is on the opposite side of the sun, Earth's gravity still has "X" effect on Jupiter.

Earth's gravity affects everything, and I mean everything, in the universe as if nothing else in the universe existed.

This, of course, is truly marvelous. It means that gravity diminishes when it does nothing and doesn't diminish when it does something!

Because we are neither addicted to sniffing the mercury fumes of the alchemical lab nor hopelessly immersed in the occult, we might want to avoid a property with such exotic characteristics, and limit ourselves to using a property where the particle has a simple affinity for other particles.

If we wanted to stick to electrical terminology, we could say that the electron has the property of moving toward a difference in potential. If this difference is represented by an absence of electrons, then the greatest potential difference will be found in the space next to the electron!

Each electron will therefore attract all other electrons!

I prefer to think of this property as the affinity propensity, where affinity is an attractive force between particles that causes them to enter into and remain in combination with one another.

Affinity propensity is the propensity of every elementary particle to occupy the space of every other elementary particle.

In this book we will be dealing almost exclusively with the effect of heat, the movement of these electrons between and among the changing potentials in the environment.

I will therefore continue with the electrical analogy.

The second property of the electron is the property to move toward a potential difference.

Thus, the two properties of the electron are as one, with the second property, its movement toward a potential difference, directing its first property, motion.

The potential difference, as we have seen, is defined as the charge. If we remove one electron from a glass rod, the glass rod has a potential difference with respect to its environment.

But the greatest possible potential difference is found in the space between the removed electron and its environment.

What happens when two electrons come together in this area of greatest potential difference, the area between the electron and the space that surrounds the electron?

The potential difference between the two combined electrons and the space around them decreases!

The area of potential difference, however, is greater.

What does this mean?

Simply put, it means that the force holding the electrons together will be used up in the process of holding the electrons together!

Electrons will continue to be attracted to the structure until the potential difference of the structure diminishes to the point that not a single additional electron will be held to the structure.

The structure itself will be spherical. Geometrically, a sphere is the most efficient structure because it has the highest volume to area ratio of any solid structure. Thus, the sphere is the smallest area that can hold the largest number of electrons, an important consideration when it is a property of the electron itself that is holding the structure of electrons together.

Thus, unlike gravity, the force that attracts electrons together and holds them together is used up in the process.

How big are electrons?

I have come to think of electrons as the basic unit of

matter. As matter occupies space, which is another word for that which we dare not name, nonexistence, then the electron need only be big enough to define nonexistence.

That isn't very big, I'm sure.   However, like all questions dealing with origin, size and demise, sizing the electron dumbs down the mind. Even if we could figure out where the first electron, or the universe for that matter, came from, how big either is, when it will all end, what would it tell us?

Nothing!

What we want to know is what's going on right here and now.

It's really kind of silly to argue about the origin of the universe when you don't even know what's making the planet your life depends on move!

What is the potential difference between the electron and the space around it?

Again, a teleological question born of the desire to name and classify that which cannot be named or classified!

The important thing to know about the electron is that every electron has the same difference in potential with the space around it.

What does this mean?

It means that any structure formed out of the electrons that is held together by their potentials differences would contain an identical number of electrons. Because the electrons would form into the most efficient structures, the structures would be identical in size, shape and residual charge.

The residual charge, strangely enough, is the charge left over after the last electron has been attracted to and become a part of the structure. The residual charge can only attract electrons into orbit around the structure.

So what do we have?

We have an elementary particle, the electron, with two properties, the property of motion, if unaffected it will travel at the speed of light, and the property of attraction, the necessity to move to and become a part of potential differences created by other electrons in the environment.

Thus, either the electron is moving toward an area where there is an absence of electrons, a potential difference, or the electron has found an area of potential difference and it has been immobilized, either into a structure of electrons or in orbiting a structure of electrons.

We have a sort of yin and yang of the real world, with opposite properties of the same particle dictating physical reality. Electrons either make up matter, or they make up electrical flows that move between potential differences in that matter.

One of the dead end concepts that result from viewing reality through mathematical equations that require balancing a limited number of terms is the mental malady of entropy, the idea that the universe was created at some time in the past, and has been running down every since.

Such ideas ignore the fact that we exist in self organizing systems, one of which is ourselves, and that if self organizing systems are all around us, there must be a self organizing system that allows atoms to come into existence.

3   The Atom

The electron is behind us, with electricity yet to come.

Those familiar with current concepts of electricity will have been short circuited by my statement that electrons move to a potential difference where the potential difference is defined as a deficit of electrons.

Electricity is currently defined as electrons moving toward a negative charge, a charge which, by definition, is produced by an excess of electrons.

Custom currently holds that electricity flows from negative to positive. This custom is left over from Benjamin Franklin's idea that fluid was moving into the glass rod when it was rubbed with a silk scarf.

So while custom permits electrons to move from negative to positive, we all know they really move from the positive to the negative charge in conductors, the conductor being what distinguishes this flow from Franklin's movement.

When we painted the end of the magnet pointing north, we called it the north pole of the magnet, the magnet being either a miniature Earth or the Earth being a gigantic magnet!

When the rule that opposites attract became reality, a matter of a couple of hundred years, someone pointed out that the painted end of the magnet couldn't be the north end of the magnet because that would mean that likes attract, and any fool knows that likes repel.

Therefore, it was agreed that it must be the unpainted, or south side of the magnet that was pointing north.

Once we know that the south ends points north, our comprehension is complete!

Actually, it is the external flows of the magnet that are lining up with the Earth's external flows.

If the electrons are exiting the north side of the magnet and moving toward the south end of the magnet, they align with the flows of electrons being emitted from the north pole of the Earth and which are also traveling south.

Thus, it is the north side of the magnet pointing north!

In fact, if you take the magnet to the north pole, the north side will point south, thereby proving that opposites do indeed attract.

Well, trying to find out which way the current flows, or which end points north could get confusing.

What does all of this have to do with explaining how the weather really works?

There are two physical occurrences that occur consistently in the environment which form the basis for understanding weather.

In order to understand how the weather really works, it is necessary to understand the processes involved in these two physical occurrences.

These initial chapters have to do with explaining these two physical occurrences.

The first of these two physical occurrences is the transference of heat within the environment.

Remember that the science of phlogiston had heat as a fluid that moved back and forth between hot and cold objects. Something actually moved out of a hot object and into a cooler object making the hotter object cooler and the cooler object hotter.

This was as good a description as any, but unfortunately, when hot objects cooled, three different things happened. They either got lighter, they got heavier or they stayed the same weight.

This didn't do too much for the idea that something was coming out of the heated object and moving into the cooling object.

When it was decided that combustion was the chemical combination of oxygen and the matter undergoing combustion, heat became an imponderable, something with no mass, to move from one quaint term to another quaint term.

Thus, some other explanation for the transfer of heat had to be devised, and what better explanation than to say that heat was motion, and that what was being transferred was motion.

That's pretty good, because motion is heat, or the definition of heat, and while transferring motion didn't tell us anything about the mechanics of the motion or the mechanics of the transfer, at least we didn't have something moving out of one thing and into another thing.

Our electron does not have mass as one of its two properties. When it comes to determining the weight of an object, then, it is indeed an imponderable.

It is not, however, an imponderable when it comes to its ability to move at the speed of light or its ability to affect and be affected by other matter as a result of its potential difference.

Because heat drives the weather, we need an understanding of why hot things make cool things hot and become less hot in the process. To get this understanding, we are going to use the electron, with its two properties, to explain how heat moves, to describe what happens when the sun hits the ground and warms the air.

The second of these two physical occurrences is the changes in air pressure that occur within the environment.

The current concepts of air pressure are derived from the process of taking a pump and compressing air.

Compressing air gives off heat.

Thus, the two physical occurrences must be connected.

Whatever physical occurrences go into the process of altering air pressure must be the same physical occurrences that results in the generation of heat!

The starting assumption for determining air pressure

would seem to be that the higher the column of air, the greater the air pressure.

This would imply that, where there is high air pressure, the air must extend further out in space.

Sunshine heats the ground, which warms the air, which in turn makes the air rise which means more air which means that on a clear day the air pressure is nice and high, pushing out all of the pesky storm clouds.

Sounds right?

Except for the fact that high air pressure is compressed air, which means less air by volume which means that the air is not warm, it's compressed so it's had the warmth removed which means that it's cold air which means that it's not being pushed out into space but rather is being pushed down from space!

Shades of which way the current travels, which end of the magnet points north.

Compressed air is cold air. It is air that has had all of the heat squished out of it during the process of compression.

Towering air masses produce low air pressure.

If air pressure is a result of the amount of air over a point, then how come towering, warm air masses produce low air pressure while lower, colder air masses produce high air pressure?

Arctic air masses move between pressure gradients as

they move south to the equator.

As a result of this isobaric intercourse, air pressure for particular air masses is not knowable.

However, on any particular day, high pressure areas denoted by clear weather are surrounded by low pressure areas, the areas that produce the weather, clouds, rain and wind.

These high pressure areas are migrating south and are what forces the warm air at the equator to rise and move north.

We are misdirecting our attention, however, by focusing on high pressure and low pressure. What we are really looking at is air temperature!

We noted that any explanation for air pressure had to use the same physical occurrences as the explanation for heat transference.

A single mechanical process has to explain both.

We know that compressing air causes air to lose heat.

It follows that removing heat will compress air!

With weather, then, we have to create an atom that will move closer to other atoms when it produces heat.

This, after all, is what we are doing when we compress air. We are forcing nuclei of atoms closer together.

The hand of God is a perfectly good scientific explanation today. Science uses it to explain what makes the planets orbit the sun, even what makes objects fall.

It is a stretch, though, to say that the palm of God compresses warm air as it moves north.   And the explanations science substitutes for God don't seem to work either. We can't say compression is a property of warm air, or that moving masses of warm air produce heat in closed systems.

Which really creates a conundrum!

Remember, phlogiston's failure, the idea that matter couldn't give off a part of itself as heat because combustion didn't produce a consistent weight loss.

Here we have a real situation. The atoms that make up the atmosphere give up heat, and exert a greater pressure.

Pressure is weight.

So the air that gives up heat becomes heavier.

Air pressure is therefore the result of the number of nuclei of atoms per volume of air rather than the height of the air.

The number of nuclei per atom is determined by the temperature of the air.

The nuclei of the atoms, therefore, move closer together as they give up heat.

What is the atom giving up that we measure as heat?

In the last chapter, we created a property in the electron which causes it to have a potential difference with the empty space around it.

This potential difference caused the electrons to occupy each other's space because it was the space closest to the electron's surface that produced the greatest potential difference.

As electrons were attracted to each other, they were held together by the potential differences between them, and as they combined into a spherical ball, the spherical ball itself had a potential difference between it and the space around it.

However, as the number of electrons increased, the potential difference of the overall structure decreased until a point was reached that the potential difference at any point on the sphere with respect to the area surrounding the sphere was not sufficient to immobilize any additional electrons which were moving in the area at their at rest speed, their property of motion.

Even though the sphere of electrons could not attract and immobilize any additional electrons, there still existed a sufficient potential difference to attract electrons. These electrons, with their at rest motion balancing the potential difference of the sphere of electrons, could move into orbit around the sphere of electrons.

The resulting structure is the classic hydrogen atom, with a single sphere of electrons forming the nucleus, and a cloud of orbiting elementary particles surrounding that nucleus.

Because it is the sphere of electrons that come together to make up the nuclei of atoms, we have to have a name for them.

In the classic atom, these spheres of electrons are what provides the atom with its weight. However, as we have seen, in the atom I am constructing, they also provide the source of attraction for the orbiting electrons, which in the classic atom is the proton.

Because these spheres of electrons serve as both neutron and proton, I have found it useful to name them units.

The only thing that we have in the nucleus, then, are these units made up of electrons coming together because of their potential differences into the spherical structure of the units all of which contain an identical number of electrons and are therefore an identical size.

The field factual congruity says that matter breaks down into its constituent elementary particles in the strongest field, and forms in the absence of a field.

This means that if you take an atom of, say iron, and put it on the surface of the sun, it will break down into its constituent units, the hydrogen and helium we see on the surface of the sun and use to conclude that the sun, and indeed the universe, is made up of hydrogen and helium atoms.

The process by which this occurs, field replacement, is the subject of Chapter Five.

Light is created when atoms break down into their constituent units, just as it is created when molecules breakdown into their constituent atoms.

Light is made up of the electrons that make up the matter that is giving off the light.

Light is merely the electrons, which have had their property of motion restrained by the potential differences of the electrons to which they are attached, regaining their at rest motion.

We could test this, but it's evidenced every day simply by turning on an electric light, or by using one of the marvelous new video cameras that convert the light back into electricity.

However, science has no use for facts unless they are predictive facts. Known facts don't prove anything.

What we are doing is inducing concepts that explain physical reality, so that it is really not surprising that the electron, with its two properties, explains reality because the two properties, matter and motion, are the basic facts of reality!

The field factual congruity says that matter releases the electrons that make it up in the strongest field available, with the field being heat, or what the matter gives off. If you put paper in fire, the paper will turn into fire.

The field factual congruity says matter forms in the absence of a field.

What type of atoms will form in the absence of a field?

The most complex atom possible.

What atom is this?

In the absence of a field, once a unit is formed, it has enough electrons to complete it, but a potential difference left over. This potential difference is sufficient to attract other electrons into orbit around it.

Electrons, however, move to areas with the greatest potential difference. The area of greatest potential difference is around other electrons.

All of the available electrons, therefore, are busy forming into units. There are none available to orbit formed units because any unit that still lacks electrons will have a greater potential difference than the completed unit, which can only attract orbiting electrons.

The excess potential difference of the unit, however, is there, and it would attract electrons if electrons were available.

Lacking available electrons, what can these units attract?

Other units, of course!

If we can visualize an area in space in which expanding light is breaking down into its individual electrons, then the electrons would immediately begin to move toward potential differences. Units would form and immediately combine with other completed units to form nuclei.

Nuclei of what?

Because every electron has the same potential difference, each unit they form is identical.

Because each unit they form is identical, each nucleus they form as a result of the remaining potential difference will be identical to every other nucleus.

This is the nucleus of the most complex atom that can form, and obviously has a somewhat greater number of units in the nucleus than atoms we find on Earth, which are atoms that have already been partially broken down in a field of combustion.

Of course, this is one hundred and eighty degrees from the current scientifically proven concept of hydrogen atoms combining in the oppressive gravitational furnaces that are the center of suns and then spewing forth in exploding novae to sprinkle the cosmos with star dust that is us, but then I'm no poet.

I'm just trying to explain the weather.

Once all of the units that can come together in the absence of a field do come together, there will still be a potential difference between the resulting nucleus and the space around it.

It is this potential difference of the nucleus that will attract the cloud of orbiting electrons when electrons become available to orbit the nucleus.

In the meantime, however, the nuclei go through the same process that the units went through.

When they can no longer attract an additional unit, and

there are no electrons available to orbit, the nuclei will attract one another.

As the nuclei come together, they form physical matter.

What physical shape do they take?

We have already seen the area with the smallest surface control the largest volume.

A sphere!

Atoms form in spheres because a sphere is the surface available for atoms to form. Matter formation occurs on the surface of the sphere of atoms as it becomes physical substance and gains volume.

The sun, Jupiter, the Earth, and other planets were all balls of matter that were forming in this manner when light from the already ignited stars making up the center of the galaxy reached sufficient strength to ignite them.

The sun became the dominate emitter, the lesser bodies, lesser emitters, with the smaller bodies cooling the fastest. How these bodies sorted themselves into orbits around the dominate emitter and lesser emitters is more fully described in Atoms, Stars and Minds.

The point here is that they do!

When the Earth combusted, the atoms at the surface began to break down, with the surface of the Earth being much like the surface of the sun as we measure it today.

With atoms with a single unit being the predominate atom on the surface of a combusting sphere, hydrogen would be an abundant atmospheric component when the surface of the Earth had cooled sufficiently to permit heavier atoms to form into a crust.

We are trying to see how giving off or absorbing heat would affect the density of air masses made up of the atoms.

We now have a concept of an atom, and we can use the hydrogen atom to see how the distance between nuclei relates to the emission or attraction of electrons, heat or cooling.

We start off with two hydrogen atoms with orbiting clouds of electrons.

We could place two hydrogen atoms next to each other so that their clouds of orbiting electrons didn't interfere one with the other.

Each atom is in perfect balance with its environment. The unit that makes up the nucleus of each has attracted all of the electrons it can attract because each electron that goes into orbit uses up some of the potential difference of the unit (remember, the definition of the property of attraction is that it is used up when it acts).

Of course, we have mentioned presence, and the orbiting electrons themselves create a potential difference at each point in their orbits that in turn attracts other orbiting electrons.

But sooner or later, we are going to have two hydrogen atoms with two nuclei each of which has a cloud of orbiting electrons.

What's going to happen when we push the two nuclei together?

If we push them together just a little, we have done something unnatural.

The nuclei of the atoms are in balance with their environment which means that they would not normally attract each other.

When we move them together, we are forcing the potential difference of each nucleus on the other.

Now, there is no potential difference between the nuclei and the space that surrounds them because the potential difference of each is being used to hold its orbiting electrons in place.

When we force the two nuclei together, we are forcing each to satisfy a portion of the other's potential difference.

We are taking a potential difference that is being satisfied by an orbiting electron and satisfying it with the nucleus of another atom.

We are replacing a portion of each of the nucleus' potential difference that is being used attracting orbiting electrons with the stationary potential difference of the other's nucleus.

More stationary potential differences replace less stationary potential differences!

This is the result of the electron's property of motion

which causes the electron to depart whenever it can. The less stationary it is, the more readily will be its departure.

The more stationary potential differences of the nuclei replace the less stationary potential differences of the orbiting electrons, and to the extent that the potential differences of the electrons are replaced by the potential differences of the nuclei, they are free to fly off into space.

These electrons are what become heat!

The closer we move the nuclei of the hydrogen atoms together, the more electrons there are that have their potential differences replaced, the more depart, and the greater the heat.

This explains why the process of compression produces heat.

If we let the two hydrogen atoms go, they will move back apart, and in the process, regain the electrons they lost, taking them out of the environment if they are available.

They move back apart because the environment requires that they maintain balance with the environment, rather than with each other. Pushing them together was placing them in disbalance with the environment.

And if we pushed them together to far?

The units themselves would come together.

With only a single nucleus, one set of orbiting electrons would no longer be necessary.

They would depart the resulting structure, blowing us to smithereens!

4   Inductance: The Pervasive Force

With atoms forming with the greatest number of units in their nuclei, and then breaking down into atoms with lesser numbers of units in their nuclei, we can see how the current concept of the atom can provide some sort of predictability with respect to chemical interactions.

If we say that a hydrogen atom has a single unit in its nucleus, and mercury has two hundred units in its nucleus, each still has a single cloud of orbiting electrons. We saw this when we blew ourselves to smithereens at the end of the last chapter. Combining units of separate atoms does away with one of the clouds of orbiting electrons, with devastating results.

The size of the cloud of orbiting electrons does not start at point "A" for the hydrogen atom, and diminish until it reaches point "B" for the mercury atoms.

The number of orbiting electrons in the cloud diminishes as the number of units increases. This continues until the number of orbiting electrons is minimal, at which point the number of electrons in the orbiting cloud once again starts at the highest number possible. As the number of units continue to increase, the number of orbiting electrons in the cloud once again begins to diminish.

The cycle of the diminishing number of electrons in the orbiting clouds repeats itself continuously as the number of units in the nuclei increases.

This is what gives elements periodicity and allows the construction of the periodic table of elements.

Atoms exist in balance with the field they occupy. This field, with respect to the Earth, is the combination of the sun's and the Earth's emission fields.

Some elements cannot exist by themselves in this field. To find stability with the field, they have to combine with atoms of other elements.

Atoms therefore have a potential difference with the environment which causes them to attract orbiting clouds of electrons.

Atoms also have a potential difference with respect to each other.

This potential difference causes them to combine with one another. Thus, whether atoms combine into molecules depends on their potential differences with their environment and with each other.

The field changes that drive the weather are the temperature changes caused by the sun. As the field changes, the potential differences between the atoms and the environment, as well as with each other, change.

Thus, atoms of hydrogen and oxygen come together depending on the differences in potential of each nucleus with the space around it, the environment, and with each other.

The fields in which the hydrogen and oxygen atoms can interact vary greatly on Earth and in its atmosphere. This accounts for the wide ranging contribution these atoms make to the weather.

The field differentials occur not only between the equator and the poles, but between sea level and the outer reaches of the atmosphere.

For purposes of this discussion, we will consider that the environmental field is such that a single hydrogen atom and a single oxygen atom will have a potential difference with respect to each other. As the two atoms are attracted to each other and come into contact, two things will happen.

First, the orbiting electrons in the cloud of each atom will interfere with the orbiting electrons in the cloud of the other atom.

The orbiting electrons will physically knock each other out of the clouds. The displaced electrons will dart off at their at rest speed in search of other potential differences.

When the nuclei lose electrons from their orbital clouds, the potential difference of the nuclei with each other increases, and the atoms will move closer together.

These are two things that are occurring, orbiting electrons are knocked out of orbit and the nuclei move closer to each other, but the two things happen as a continuous process until the interference of the orbiting electrons with one another is not sufficient to overcome the hold of the nuclei on those electrons.

At this point, the two nuclei are held together by the potential difference between them, but maintained apart by the interference of their orbital clouds with each other.

This is the classic concept of dynamic equilibrium that is used to explain how matter is held together, but with a twist.

Classic atoms with like charges in the nuclei repelled each other, leaving up in the air any explanation how orbiting electrons held the repellent atoms together.

The atom constructed out of the electron with its two opposing properties provides a physical description of dynamic equilibrium that supports the physical matter that results from atoms and molecules crystallizing into physical matter.

When the hydrogen and oxygen atoms reach a point at which their potential differences with each other and the environment are in balance, the stability of the resulting molecular structure is only as good as the stability of the field in which it forms.

No matter how much the potential difference holds the nuclei together, the molecules would be continually breaking apart with the smallest change in temperature, the slightest variation in the field in which they exist.

In fact, a change in the field might cause the molecules, made up of a single hydrogen atom and a single oxygen atom to have a potential difference sufficient to attract an additional hydrogen atom!

This additional hydrogen atom would then burrow itself into place the same way the first two atoms came together, but this time the environmental conditions are such that the resulting water molecule falls to the ground.

These molecules of water, containing two hydrogen atoms and one oxygen atom, happen to be stable on the surface of the Earth at this particular time in the Earth's evolution. The surface field permits water's stability.

If the Earth's surface happened to carry the temperature of, say, Venus, then the molecular structure could not exist.

This atom is descriptive, and as such, does not do what the modern magicians of science demand, predict. But then, I'm not too sure how much predicting structured orbital shells did. I think that putting the electron in orbit was sufficient to open the mind so that it could draw relationships from the information gleaned from arranging the elements in a periodic table according to physical characteristics.

Because weight is a product of the number of units in the nucleus of the atom, and because the overall potential difference of the nucleus, the size of the atom's cloud of orbiting electrons, varies with the same number, one of the physical characteristics that emerge from arranging atoms on the periodic table is electrical potential.

Predictive science, on the other hand, is more like our

Hollywood concept of the shaman in some D. W. Griffith epic or perhaps King Arthur's court, raising his hand just as the solar eclipse casts the world into darkness, and then assigning the ability to predict to some sort of magical power of numbers or incantations.

We don't have to predict regular physical occurrences because regular physical occurrences occur on a regular basis.

And predicting something that we don't know exists results in creating something in our recall that may or may not exist in reality, but which will be found soon enough in reality regardless of whether or not it exists in reality.

Today, of course, everybody is running around looking for facts that don't exist while studiously ignoring those that do!

Saying that a hypothesis predicts a fact is simply saying that the picture of reality that the hypothesis paints has a hole in it.

The order in which the elements of a picture are found does not validate the picture. It is the picture, itself, the cohesiveness of its elements, that provides comprehension.

If the picture is meaningless, no amount of predictive twaddle can make it real.

Here, we just want to take what we know, the facts that make up the picture, and explain them in the simplest possible fashion.

The idea that electrons orbit the nucleus of the atom

because the nucleus of the atom has a potential difference between it and the space around it is a simple explanation that we will carry right on through our total discussion of how the weather occurs, why the formation of ice dumps tons of heat into the environment, why the formation of hydrogen and oxygen atoms into water molecules absorbs heat and how water breaks down under the sun.

We have seen that the electron has a potential difference with the space around it and that this potential difference causes electrons to come together into units.

We have seen that these units have a potential difference with the space around them, and that this potential difference causes them to combine into nuclei of atoms.

We have seen that the nuclei have a potential difference with the space around them, and that this potential difference attracts electrons into orbits around them.

These orbits, because the nucleus is spherical, are random with respect to orientation.

This means that they go every which way.

Under what circumstances would the orbits align themselves so that their planes would be parallel?

Reviewing all of the ways the electron, with its two properties, can appear in reality will lead us to the answer to this question.

The electron has a property of motion which causes it

to move toward potential differences, its second property.

Electrons can be ambient, moving among and between potential differences in the environment without actually being attached to a potential difference.

Electrons can be directed.

Flows of directed electrons occur in two instances.

The first type of directed flow is a flow of electrons between potential differences. The environment might create the potential difference, or we might fashion the potential difference. The result is the same, an electrical flow.

The second type of directed flow is the flow of electrons directed by combustion, the formation of the electromagnetic structure in which the electron's motion is balanced by the potential differences holding the structure together.

Electrons can be stationary, their motion captured and restrained by their potential differences, the unit that makes up the nucleus of an atom.

Finally, as in the current discussion, electrons can balance their motion with specific potential differences.

This can occur in two ways.

The first is when they randomly orbit the spherical nucleus of an atom to create an orbiting cloud of electrons.

The second is when they orbit a directed flow of electrons, either electricity or light.

So we have electrons appearing as ambient, directed, stationary and balanced. Directed electrons are either electricity or light. Balanced electrons are either orbital clouds or inductances.

We've encountered the term presence in this discussion.

Presence is the existence of a single elementary particle at all points in a continuous flow of elementary particles. The single particle is not the same particle, but because all electrons are identical, it might as well be the same particle.

At every point in a flow of electrons there is an electron that has just left the point and an electron that has just entered the point.

Because the electron is the most basic particle, the building block of all matter, there is no way that we can measure it, other than indirectly by its effect. Therefore, we have no way of holding it in place in order to examine how its potential difference might effect other electrons.

However, by examining a flow of electrons, we can treat any point in the flow as if it were a stationary electron.

What do we know about the potential difference of an electron?

Electrons move to where there is a potential difference.

Thus, a single electron, with a potential difference, will attract other electrons causing them to move toward the potential difference.

If there were no field, no flow of electrons in the area, electrons moving toward each other's potential differences would result in matter formation, the electrons forming units, the units forming nuclei, the nuclei becoming atoms, the atoms becoming matter.

However, this is not the case with a flow of electrons. While the effect of the electron can be felt at any point in the flow, just as if there was always an electron at that point, the fact of the matter is, the electron that produces the potential difference at any point in the flow has long departed by the time other electrons are attracted to the point.

There is no way that one electron can combine with another electron when the other electron is a part of a flow of electrons!

This is the first part of the field factual congruity, matter forms in the absence of a field. The presence of a field, a flow of electrons, prevents electrons from forming into matter.

The absence of specific electrons in the flow with which ambient electrons, electrons which are available in the environment, can combine, does not prevent the flow from attracting these electrons.

There is still a potential difference at each point in the flow, and that potential difference attracts electrons out of the ambient field.

And, just as electrons orbit the potential difference of the nucleus of an atom, so will they orbit potential differences at all points in a flow of electrons.

Because electrons will attempt to orbit the flow at all points in the flow, the only electrons that can orbit the flow are those that orbit at right angles to the flow. To orbit in anything but a circle at right angles to the flow would result in interference with other particles orbiting the flow. Interference would knock other particles out of the flows, permitting only those particles orbiting at right angles.

This, of course, is how electrical inductance is measured.

The direction of the inductive flow is determined by pointing the thumb of the right hand in the direction of the flow. The direction in which the fingers curl is the direction of the inductive flow.

The source of the right hand rule, which also governs motion in the solar system, is complex, but is found in the only other non symmetrical phenomena in the universe, the fact that once ignition occurs, combustion proceeds as a cooling process, a cycle in which the heating leg of the cycle is always an infinitesimal amount smaller than the cooling cycle.

We can also see orbiting electrons doing the interfering we talked about when we described atoms forming into molecules.

Because inductive flows always move at right angles to

the direction of the flows, we can try to force two conductors with flows moving in opposite directions together.

The opposing flows attempt to push the conductors apart, which is what the flows in atoms try to do with their nuclei when their nuclei attract each other.

When the currents are traveling in the same direction, the inductances combine the flows, which in turn move the conductors together, a phenomena that provides the basis for the mechanism that regulates the uniform expansion of the electromagnetic spectrum.

Inductive flows are proportional to the flow of electrons the inductive flows orbit.

If we take a single flow of electrons, we will have a proportional flow of orbiting electrons. A flow of electrons one electron thick would produce an orbital flow one electron thick. The inductive flow is a primary flow that induces the secondary flow of electrons one electron thick.

Double the primary flow and you double the inductive flow.

When electrons combine to make up the units of the nuclei of atoms, the potential differences are used up holding the structure together. Why does the inductive flow, an orbital flow around the primary flow, double?

Because the electrons are not orbiting another electron. They are orbiting the effect of an electron which is no longer present!

As a result, the potential difference is satisfied only when it exists, and it always exists in full at any point in a flow of electrons.

Thus, the rule of inductance is that it is proportional to the primary flow of electrons.

We have been using an imaginary flow of electrons, with occasional reference to electrical flows.

Electrical flows, which we will cover more completely when we get to the chapter on electricity, can be man-made. When we make flows of electrons, we really do a bang up job. We produce gigantic flows to satisfy our need for the flows to produce work.

Flows in nature are much smaller, and generally go undetected. For instance, the surface of the Earth is made up of elements with potential differences among them, and many of those elements lie contiguous to each other. Normally, we would think that the potential differences between elements on Earth would dissipate, like a shorted battery, after a period of time.

However, temperature, the field in which the matter exists, determines the electrical potential of the matter, both with respect to the field, and with respect to other elements.

Therefore, the fact that the Earth rotates on its axis in front of a combusting body, the sun, means that the potential differences of the elements on the Earth's surface are constantly changing with respect to their environment and with respect to one another.

Where there are potential differences, there are flows of electrons.

The Earth is host to electrical flows, although they are difficult to measure and are dwarfed by the electron flows that move between it surface and its atmosphere.

Additionally, there are electron flows between potential differences in the atmosphere.

However, by far the most important flows of electrons with respect to the weather are the directed flows created by the sun's combustion process.

The electrons that make up the inductive flows of the sun's rays are important in weather because, as the Earth rotates in front of the sun, the need for electrons to establish these inductive flows starts at sunrise.

With sunset, the electrons, no longer necessary to balance the primary flows of the sun's rays, become ambient in the atmosphere.

The current concept of light has it resulting from alternately collapsing electrical and magnetic fields which induce the flow of the light at right angles to the collapsing fields.

This rather forced concept, which is designed to accommodate Young's fallacious conclusion that light's ability to create interference patterns requires that light be analogous to, and travel like water waves, can be replaced by the simple concept of light as a flow of electrons.

The flows expand over the surface of the sphere available for their expansion, but, like the light in Young's experiment, the flows are overexpanding.

Because we know that light does not overexpand, but rather expands uniformly, something is keeping it from overexpanding.

That something is the inductive flows!

In Young's experiment, light is passed through two slits, and in the process, the center of expansion is changed, causing the light to overexpand. If the slits are the same distance from the light, the overexpansion in the resulting spheres is identical. When the light in these overexpanded spheres is intermingled, the inductive flows recombine the overexpanded light. When the recombined light is collected on a screen, all of the light is present, but it is in bands because there is no light in the areas out of which the light has been recombined.

The continual process of light's uniform expansion being regulated by inductive flows recombining the overexpansion constitutes a mechanism at any point in an expanding sphere of light which produces a force back toward the source of the light, the force of attraction we define as gravity. It can be seen that, because the inductive flows that produce the mechanism are proportional to the light at any point, and the strength of the light is inversely proportional to its distance from its source, the mechanism of attraction also diminishes inversely from the source of the expanding electromagnetic spectrum in which it is embedded.

The only importance that this mechanism has in our consideration of how the weather works is that it works on the individual units that make up the nuclei of atoms. If an atom has one unit in the nucleus, then it will take one unit of force to move it against the effect of this mechanism.

However, if an atom has sixteen units in the nucleus, then it will take sixteen units of force to move the atom against the effect of this mechanism, because the atom will have sixteen mechanisms working on it at the same time.

This is how we determine weight, and organize elements accordingly.

On the other hand, the hydrogen and oxygen atom would each fall toward the source of attraction at the same rate regardless of the number of units in the nucleus of either atom because each unit has only one mechanism acting on it, no matter how many units are tied together in the nucleus.

The real effect of inductive flows with respect to the electromagnetic spectrum, light, is found in their existence.

Or, perhaps this is better stated, in their nonexistence!

Before the sun rises over the horizon, there are no inductances with respect to light because there is no light.

The electrons in the environment are doing any of a number of things.

They are making up nuclei of atoms. They are making up clouds of electrons orbiting the nuclei of atoms. They are ambient in the environment, electrons that are moving with respect to no specific difference of potential.

There are also electrons making up the magnetic flows of the Earth, whose rotation acts like a continually changing inductive field inducing an external flow of electrons exiting the north pole, traveling around the Earth and re-entering it at the south pole.

There are electrons externally orbiting magnets, and a lot of electrons being used in service to the needs of civilization.

When the sun peeks over the horizon, and the first rays of light enter this environment, the flows are going to establish potential differences at every point in the flows.

These potential differences are going to compete in the environment for electrons.

Any electrons in the environment that are ambient, will, of course, be available to orbit the flows.

Other electrons will become available because the flows of light will have a sufficient potential difference to attract them from what they are doing to form the inductive flows around the flows of light.

None of these sources, however, would be sufficient to provide the massive number of electrons that the light from the rising sun will demand form into inductive flows. If the electrons aren't available, the light will overexpand

and break down to provide the electrons.

And the potential difference of the flows with their environment would not be sufficient to attract electrons out of, say, the grass lawn around your swimming pool, let alone from the swimming pool itself.

How, then, do the sun's rays get the electrons they need to establish the inductive flows that allow them to maintain their coherence?

By field replacement!

Field replacement is the dominate process by which heat is transferred between elements of the environment.

It dictates the movement of electrons between the Earth and the atmosphere, and thus, controls the movement of air masses in the atmosphere.

5   Field Replacement: The Result of Combustion

Let's see if I can get this right.

On the surface of the sun there is an atom. It is probably helium, because this is the most common atom in the infinite universe. This scientific fact is known with unerring certainty because that's what we see on the surface of the sun!

This helium atom has two electrons in orbit around its nucleus. However, with all of the activity going on around it on the surface of the sun, one of the electrons jumps to another orbital level. How it does this is a mystery, but it does, as is proven by the fact that it emits a quantity of radiation in the process.

Now, like which way the magnet points, or whether electricity flows to the negative or the positive, we don't want to confuse ourselves with the question whether the new orbit is further away from the nucleus, or closer to the nucleus. We'll just say that it moves further away from the nucleus because the atom is now less active, has less motion, and if the orbit is larger, then the electron must be going slower. Or, is it the opposite, because if the orbit is larger, and the electron is moving at the same rate, then its going faster, and there is more movement.

Hmmm.

Well, let's not worry about it now becuase when the radiation gets to where it's going, we'll know exactly what happened.

And that's what this little quantity of radiation does, travel the ninety three million miles through space, passes through the atmosphere quite miraculously, and gets to where its going, the surface of the Earth.

And lands in a pond!

Now, the pond is made up of hydrogen and oxygen atoms held together in water molecules.

They are held together by the well understood force of molecular attraction, a close cousin to the molecular magnets that are used to explain magnetism.

In this pond, some ninety three million miles from the point that the electron orbiting the helium atom on the sun changed orbit, the quantity of light strikes the water molecule, changing the orbit of an orbiting electron in the water molecule.

We know exactly in which direction the orbit changes this time. It is exactly opposite the change that occurred in the helium atom on the surface of the sun!

If you think this all sounds passingly silly, you apparently are not steeped in the mathematical systems that makes such conceptualizations reasonable to supposedly sensible minds.

And I don't even mention that these electrons are actually wave particles, or perhaps, particle waves that have no place in space and time. But, then, this is the physicist's atom, while the atom that we have been using in the last several chapters is the chemist's atom.

But then, the physicist seeks to elucidate light, whereas the lowly chemist is concerned only with the physical interaction caused by noble light's progeny, heat.

As they say about domains, when in Rome...

But I'm not in Rome!

As we all know, we cannot see the universe unless we are traveling on the rapidly moving rod of chalk that marks the boundaries of the known universe in symbols devised by human genius.

When we complain that mathematics lead us to concepts that are just plain silly at best, and downright ridiculous the rest of the time, we are told that without spending a lifetime submerged in the liturgical symbolism of the craft, we cannot expect to see the elegance of the process.

Elegance? Isn't that beauty's upper class cousin, and, like beauty, in the eye of the beholder? How do you see elegance, we ask, in attempting to explain why the water in the dam pond evaporates?

And we get the Vanderbilt answer, the epitome of elitism, that if we have to ask, we can't afford it, only in this case, its not a question of being among the rich, but rather of being among the anointed.

So, to follow elegance blindly, these little packets of radiation, produced by the change in the orbital level of electrons in helium atoms on the surface of the sun, travel to the pond and, striking the molecules, get them all excited.

The molecules, as a result of ubiquitous intermolecular forces, begin to jump around at random. Sometimes they get so energetic that they burst the bounds of the watery surface and jump into the atmosphere, evaporate. The higher the temperature, the more energetic these little devils get, and the more of them escape into the surrounding air, increasing the atmospheric water content.

And, of course, condensation is the opposite of evaporation, so that when these water molecules get tired, they turn into rain!

The concept of motion, which replaced the phlogistic idea that heat had substance which moved from a hot object to a cold object, is not really that bad. It's just not much different than the transfer of heat or, in the case of electricity, fluid from one place to another. With heat, phlogiston is transferred, with electricity, a sort of philosophical fluid was transferred, and here, motion is transferred.

All of these explanations have one thing in common.

None of the three explain anything!

They all have another thing in common.

They all have it backward!

All of this radiation coming in the form of sunlight, all these quanta or packets, or whatever, are supposed to warm up the ground. Thus, the radiation is stored in the ground as motion, and as long as the sun is up, the motion is refreshed.

However, as soon as the sun goes down, the impetus for this motion is no longer present, and the motion subsides. The intermolecular subsidence has, I guess, the electrons returning to their former orbits, and in the process, re-radiating the bits and pieces of radiation quanta back into space from whence they came.

This is the basis for the idea of the thermal balance of the planet. Under this scientifically measurable notion, the Earth's incoming radiation exactly balances its outgoing radiation, with the outgoing heat from the Earth's internal combustion process exactly equal to the incoming starlight so that the thermal balance equation balances.

To really understand heat, let's do the same thing with an atom and an electron flow that we did with the two nuclei of hydrogen atoms in Chapter Three.

Both the nucleus of an atom and a flow of electrons produce stationary potential differences.

When we moved the stationary potential differences of the hydrogen atoms together, the non stationary orbiting electrons were replaced by the potential differences of the two nuclei satisfying each other.

We saw this effect with compression and, by moving the potential differences of two nuclei in closer proximity, we are simulating field replacement.

Actual field replacement involves replacing the

electrons in the orbiting clouds with a field, the stationary potential differences in a flow of electrons.

In field replacement, the nucleus' need for orbiting electrons is replaced with the presence of a field!

The nucleus of a hydrogen atom has enough orbiting electrons in the cloud to balance the potential difference it has with the space around it.

If there were nothing else in the universe but this hydrogen atom, a single unit made up of all of the electrons that can come together without being able to hold stationary a single additional electron, and there were just enough electrons in existence to be attracted into orbit around the nucleus, and no more, then what we would have is a perfectly balanced hydrogen atom.

All of the electrons' property of motion is being used up to move those electrons toward all of the potential differences of all of the electrons in the hydrogen atom.

The structure is in perfect balance, with the two forces that make up the opposing properties of electrons that make it up exactly in balance.

Looking at this idealistic picture, we can make a conclusion.

No matter what happens to this hydrogen atom, it will at all times attempt to reach this ideal state.

The universe may be in a state of constant conflict, but the conflict is an attempt to reach a balance between the opposing properties of the elementary particle we have styled the electron!

To demonstrate field replacement, we are going to disrupt this perfect hydrogen atom, just as ignition and combustion disrupt the balance of matter with its environment, keeping the universe in constant turmoil, and in my opinion, at least, development.

We are going to take a single flow of electrons and pass it by some distance from the atom.

We have positioned the flow of electrons far enough away from the atom so that it has no effect on the atom.

The nucleus of the atom has attracted a cloud of orbiting electrons.

Now we mentally move the flow toward the atom, and position it so that it is as far away from the nucleus as the orbiting electron with the largest orbit.

What is going to happen to that outermost electron?

The outermost electron could move to the potential difference that results from the presence of the flow of electrons.

But that's not the field replacement we want to illustrate.

The outermost electrons might be knocked out of orbit by collision with the electrons in the flow, but that is not field replacement either.

The outermost orbiting electron was the last electron that the potential difference of the nucleus could attract.

When that electron went into orbit around the nucleus, there was no more potential difference between the nucleus and the space around it, and therefore there was no potential difference toward which an electron could move.

When we moved the flow of electrons next to the orbiting cloud, we replaced the potential difference of the nucleus being satisfied, or used up, by the outermost orbiting electron with the potential difference that existed in the flow.

The potential difference in the flow of electrons is stationary.

The potential difference of the outermost electron is non stationary.

Stationary potential differences in the environment replace non stationary potential differences.

This is the result of placing opposing properties in the same particle.

Potential differences overcome motion.

Thus, if there is a stationary potential difference, the property of motion dictates the extent to which a particular electron can satisfy a stationary potential difference.

If the stationary potential difference is merely balancing an electron's property of motion, the intervention of another stationary potential difference will allow the electron's motion to overcome its potential difference, and the electron will fly off into space.

Thus, a flow of electrons, having stationary potential differences at every point in the flow, will replace electrons in the orbiting cloud of an atom.

A flow of electrons is a field, and thus a field replaces orbiting electrons.

To what extent will a flow of electrons, the field, replace orbiting electrons?

If we double the flow of electrons next to the hydrogen atom, we double the number of electrons that are replaced. Thus, the same physical effect that applies to inductance applies to field replacement.

Field replacement is proportional to the field.

At this point, I would like to interject a note on terminology.

An orbiting electron is moving toward the potential difference of the nucleus.

This movement is the result of the potential difference of the electrons that make up the nucleus and the potential difference of the orbiting electrons.

Because we defined the force of attraction that results from the electron's property of moving toward potential differences as a property that can be used up, then to the extent that the electron is held in orbit, its property of motion is using up a portion of the potential difference in both the orbiting electron and the nucleus.

A nucleus that has a potential difference with its

environment can thus be considered to have an excess potential difference.

This excess potential difference, which is also found in the electron, is what we measure as a charge.

Thus, we can say that orbiting electrons satisfy the excess potential difference of a nucleus, or we can say that orbiting electrons are using up the excess potential difference of the nucleus.

When the stationary presence of a field replaces the orbiting electrons, we can say that the orbiting electrons took off, regained their motion, because the excess potential difference of the nucleus was satisfied by the stationary potential difference of the field.

On the other hand, when the field is removed, the nucleus has an excess potential difference which will attract electrons into orbit until the excess potential difference is used up.

We ignored the fact that the outermost electron would move to the flow of electrons because of the flow's presence, and the resulting stationary potential difference.

The primary flow of electrons has to establish an inductive flow.

Therefore, the electron that is liberated by the flow is immediately attracted to and becomes a part of the inductive flow.

Replaced electrons become a part of the inductive flows of the flows of electrons that replaced them!

What about the hydrogen atom's need for balance?

As long as the flow is present, the flow will balance the potential difference of the nucleus, and the atom will be in perfect balance with its environment.

What happens when we remove the flow?

The potential difference of the nucleus reappears, and it attempts to capture back the electron that departed, which it can, because the flow which it is orbiting is no longer in the environment.

Now that's elegant!

The field comes into existence and replaces orbiting electrons in the atoms it affects. However, the field itself requires those electrons to establish inductive flows.

When the field departs, it leaves ambient electrons in the environment and atoms with excess potential difference toward which those electrons wish to move.

When the sun comes up, light strikes a rock. The light that doesn't reflect off of the rock, moves between the clouds of orbiting electrons that make up the surface of the rock, replacing orbiting electrons.

Those orbiting electrons, no longer needed to maintain the balance of the atoms that make up the rock, depart into the atmosphere.

However, the atmosphere has a field, flows of sunlight, that it didn't have prior to the sun coming up.

These primary flows need inductive flows to balance

them, because all potential differences in the environment seek balance.

The sun, through the process of field replacement, is liberating a bunch of electrons into the environment. The flows of electrons that make up the light need a bunch of electrons to balance their presence.

The liberated electrons become the inductive flows that regulate the light's expansion!

So instead of the Earth absorbing radiation, whatever that is, in the morning, and giving it up in the evening, the Earth is giving off vast quantities of electrons in the morning, particles with a potential difference with the space they occupy, and, you guessed it, in the evening, taking them back, sometimes violently in the form of lightning.

Now, a lot is happening with this process. In the morning, flowers and trees open up to the sky, the better to provide conduits for the electrons streaming skyward. We have to remember that the very existence of the sunlight creates a potential difference with the atoms of atmosphere through which they flow. The sun's rays are going to rob those atoms of electrons from their orbiting clouds to the extent they can. This in turn is going to affect the relationship of the atoms with each other, and overall, the relationship of the atmosphere with the ground.

Whether the sunlight reaches the ground or not, the atmosphere is going to hug the ground attempting to pull electrons out of the orbiting clouds of the atoms that make it up.

At night, the flowers and trees are going to close up in self protection, attempting to block the ambient electrons in the atmosphere, a population of electrons that really becomes a bunch as the sun's rays depart, leaving the electrons that made up the inductive flows to dart around in an environment which no longer has potential differences other than the potential differences of the ambient electrons and the need of the Earth for electrons to rebalance the atoms disbalanced by the flows from the departing sun.

When we look at what is happening when the sun's rays hit the surface of the water, we see something very interesting. Instead of intermolecular forces and energetic molecules, we see hydrogen and oxygen atoms held together by the potential differences in their nuclei, but kept apart by the interference of the electrons in their orbiting clouds. The ratio of hydrogen atoms to oxygen atoms is about two to one. As the sun's rays hit the surface of the water, the electrons in the orbiting clouds are replaced to the extent of the flow's presence.

While the sun's rays replace these orbiting electrons, and in doing so maintain the individual atom's balance with its environment, they also replace the potential differences holding the nuclei together.

The attraction resulting from the potential differences of the nuclei was being countered by the interference of the orbiting clouds.

As field replacement occurs on the surface of the water, orbiting electrons depart, eliminating the interference, but the field replaces the potential differences of the nuclei, allowing them to move apart. (Where the orbiting electrons are removed as a result of the absence of a field, the nuclei move together into a physical structure, ice.)

As the field replacement causes the nuclei to move apart, the surface of the water becomes unstable.

Hydrogen is lighter than, and non reactive with the nitrogen that predominates the atmospheric environment and it quickly departs the surface of the water, pushed up by the weight of the atmosphere around it. It doesn't stay around to recombine with the oxygen.

The oxygen, having no connection with the water, and being only slightly heavier than the nitrogen, with which it is also non reactive, becomes a part of the atmosphere.

Over time, the surface of the water diminishes as the molecules of water break down into their constituent atoms.

If the sun's rays were not striking water, but rather were hitting the earth part of the Earth, the result would be somewhat different.

The idea that the Earth gives up heat when the sun comes up, and takes it in when the sun goes down is counterintuitive.

I really hate to use that term, because it is the phrase that is used to justify every fantasy, and beyond, that modern science seeks to make reality.

However, we do tend to think of the Earth getting warmer under the sun, and growing colder when the sun departs, and we do this because we get warm when the sun comes up, and cold when it goes down.

The reason that we get warm when the sun comes up, however, is that we are being bathed in the electrons being emitted from the Earth. When the sun goes down, we are being deprived of the electrons, they are being pulled out of the atmosphere, and the atmosphere is pulling them out of our skin.

We can see this effect on our flesh. There is an old parlor trick in which the victim is blindfolded, and told he is going to be burned. A piece of ice is then used to create the sensation. The victim can't tell the difference between hot and cold sensations.

The reason is that the same thing is happening on the surface of the skin when both hot and cold are applied. Heat will cause the electrons that are holding the molecules of skin together to depart the surface of the skin as a result of field replacement.

Ice, having a deficit of electrons in its structure, pulls the electrons directly out of the skin.

Both leave a "burn".

So counterintuitive or no, the effect of the sun striking the Earth is opposite the way we think the sun works.

We think that the sun radiates, and the radiation is

absorbed by the Earth.

In reality, the emissions from the sun, the sun's field, replace electrons in the atoms and molecules of atoms on the surface of the Earth, allowing them to be emitted into the atmosphere.

We think that the Earth re-radiates the radiation it has absorbed when the sun goes down.

In reality, the atoms and molecules of atoms, robbed of the stationary potential differences provided by the presence of the sun's emission field have a potential difference, when the sun goes down, that draws the electrons out of the atmosphere.

The sun's emission field, fortunately, needs all of these emitted electrons to form inductive flows around the sun's emissions as they pass through the atmosphere.

Electrons always move toward potential differences. Potential differences are produced by a lack of electrons rather than by an increase of electrons. If potential differences were created by an excess of electrons, then as soon as two electron came together, it would be all over for the universe. Two electrons would have more potential difference than one electron, and thus attract twice as many electrons, which, when attracted, would attract as many more. The process would continue until all of the electrons in the universe were clumped together in a single charged pile.

It is only by thinking in terms of deficits of electrons

creating greater potential differences which can only be satisfied by the potential differences of other electrons which move toward potential differences in the environment that we can correctly analyze the weather, and, for that matter, physical reality.

The breakdown of molecules of water under the sun, however, has a somewhat different effect than when the sun merely strikes crystalline matter on the surface of the Earth.

When the molecule of water formed out of individual atoms of oxygen and hydrogen, the atoms gave up electrons from their orbital clouds into the environment as a result of the nuclei moving together.

When the molecule of water breaks down, the individual atoms recapture electrons out of the environment.

Thus, when water "evaporates" on the surface of your skin, it is pulling electrons out of the environment, which includes your skin and the air around your skin.

The result is that the breakdown cools the area in which it occurs.

The breakdown of molecules on the surface of water by the process of field replacement doesn't seem to have much analogy to boiling water.

In boiling water, the heat at the bottom of the pan breaks down the hydrogen and oxygen into individual atoms. As the oxygen and hydrogen atoms are both lighter than the water, they form bubbles which rise to the surface.

When they break out of the surface, however, they run into the environmental conditions which allowed them to combine in the first place.

Matter exists in the field that permits its existence!

When the sun hits the surface of water, the field that is produced does not permit the water to exist.

The hydrogen atoms are pushed away from the surface of the water before nightfall creates conditions that would permit the hydrogen and oxygen atoms to reform into water molecules.

However, the environmental conditions above the surface of the boiling water are the same conditions that let the water exist before the heat was applied.

The oxygen and hydrogen atoms immediately begin forming together into water molecules, and the steam over the boiling water is created.

When the water molecules break down on the surface of the ocean, more particularly the equatorial oceans, and the hydrogen atoms are pushed into the atmosphere, what happens to the oxygen?

It's heavier than its surrounding nitrogen, so it's separated from the hydrogen atoms.

How does it catch up with the hydrogen atoms so that it can reform into the ice like crystals we call clouds?

6   Combustion: The Source of Field Replacement

We don't hear much about it nowadays, but phlogiston ruled the world for about three centuries.

Phlogiston is a concept of combustion, and the reason that something about combustion could rule the world is that, as in the mythology of fire being given to mankind, combustion is pretty omnipresent.

Phlogiston held that when an object was burning, it gave up a part of itself, and that part went into other matter that was warming up.

Newton, however, explained weight by placing the attractive force into the matter that had the weight, in effect, weight causing itself!

As a result, we began to think of weight as intrinsic to matter rather than thinking of weight as the result of an external force, something acting on the matter.

We lost sight of the fact that weight is merely an expression of the force it takes to move matter against a field of attraction and began to think of weight as the field of attraction itself.

Thus, if something that was burning was giving up what made it up, because the matter had weight, what it gave up must have weight.

In true scientific fashion, it became obvious that all that was necessary to prove the existence or nonexistence of phlogiston was to weigh the matter before it was heated, and weigh it after it was heated, in fact weigh it throughout the whole process.

If the matter got lighter, then phlogiston would be proven.

If it didn't, then we could start to ridicule the concept of phlogiston, but better, we could laugh at anyone suggesting that anything like phlogiston might be valid.

This is a time honored tradition in science. Aristotle, for instance, had an abiding interest in what made objects move. His explanation of why celestial objects move involved having them revolve around the Earth.

When Galileo sought to show the accuracy of the Copernican system, with its sun centered solar system, it wasn't sufficient to say, well, the sun doesn't revolve around the Earth, and neither do the darn planets, so what is making the planets, including the Earth, move?

It was necessary to say that Aristotle, and all of the mental midgets that think his way, and by think his way, think anything he thought, is just dog poop, and the correct way to think is that the Earth goes around the sun, and that's a fact!

This sort of process, where the only way to discredit individual concepts is to discredit the reputation of the concept's proponent, led to Newton, who considered the question of why planets move so inconsequential that he left it up to God to push them along in their orbits.

And, of course, our own explanation, that motion in closed systems is conserved, is even more asinine. It seeks to hide the fact that we don't know diddlysquat about what is making the planets move while at the same time avoiding saying what we are really saying, that God makes them move.

We protect our ignorance with some mumbo jumbo so that if anyone questions our ignorance we can all point fingers at him and laugh uproariously.

Of course, the people that wished to discredit phlogiston believed fervently in the mass/gravity concept, so much so that to them mass was a total reality.

There was no reason to think that what matter gave up in combustion had no mass, or even that the concept of mass was probably the most successful piece of mumbo jumbo ever articulated.

And they also knew that the process of combustion resulted in three different outcomes with respect to the matter combusted. The matter got heavier, it got lighter, or it didn't change weight at all.

What kind of conclusion do these results support?

That what is given off in the process of combustion is nothing, an imponderable, light, the will of the wisp, the essence of thought!

As these guys warmed themselves around the bonfire made out of all of the books that used phlogiston to explain combustion, and that is no joke, they proposed the chemical theory of combustion.

It had been determined that agents could produce chemical changes in matter.

Combustion, then, was simply the agent oxygen and the combustible matter undergoing chemical combination!

What could be clearer?

After all, nothing burned without oxygen. That was clear by trying to burn something in a vacuum. And if something burned in a vacuum, why we could just assume that oxygen was present.

Else, how could it burn in a vacuum?

Science can always assume that which has been determined to be scientific fact!

Once we accept the chemical theory of combustion, we are cut off from explaining how sunlight might break down molecules on the surface of water because the molecule doesn't break down. It is not combining with oxygen, it is already oxygen.

Which makes you wonder where the fire was that created the oceans.

On the other end of the scale, we can't explain what is happening on the surface of the sun in terms of combustion because there is no oxygen on the surface of the sun, just hydrogen and helium.

Thus, we have to come up with some exotic, counterintuitive, even preposterous explanation that has the sun being an oversized hydrogen bomb, where its elements are combining in the interior rather than breaking down on the surface.

Combustion is important in understanding weather because it is on one end of the field factual congruity, which is basically a statement about field replacement.

A factual congruity is really what the mind does. We are reasoning people because we can take two separate facts and make them into a single fact. We can put a horn on a horse and create the myth of the unicorn.

This ability allows us to understand things in the environment that are actually two facts in one.

There are not a whole lot of these, but two of the most obvious are that objects accelerate as they fall in a field, gravity if you will, and light diminishes as it expands.

In each case we have two facts that are always present together.

Another factual congruity can be made out of these two factual congruities. Because the rate at which objects fall is the same rate at which light diminishes, an inverse square rate, and one mirrors the other, we could recognize that objects fall in an expanding sphere of light.

We can carry this one step further, then, and say that because the closer matter gets to combusting matter, the greater becomes its own propensity for bursting into flame and undergoing combustion, that matter exists in the field produced by combustion to the extent that the field permits the matter to exist.

This principle, the field factual congruity, drives weather systems because when the sun comes up, certain combinations of matter cannot exist in certain areas of the environment.

The molecules on the surface of water are an example of this statement.

But it is not the statement of the field factual congruity that is important in understanding weather, but rather it is the understanding of the combustion process itself that provides the understanding of how heat flows in the environment.

The best way to describe the combustion process is to use two phosphorus matches.

We have seen how compressing the nuclei of two atoms gives off heat. The nuclei satisfy the potential differences that were being satisfied by orbiting electrons prior to compression. The orbiting electrons, no longer needed, fly off into space, and can be measured as activity, or heat.

When we strike a match, we are physically tearing atoms apart from each other. The nuclei of the atoms, when combined together, were satisfying each other's potential differences. When we tear them apart with friction, we create a need in the recently asundered atoms for orbiting clouds of electrons. When the electrons rush in, they replace the remaining existing fields and ignite the atoms.

What is ignition?

Let's go back to the atom, with an orbiting cloud of electrons, and a flow of electrons passing by.

The presence of the flow of electrons will replace electrons in the orbiting cloud, and will do so in proportion to the number of electrons in the flow.

This is field replacement.

Now, instead of having a single atom next to the flow, let's line up ten thousand atoms in a row next to the flow.

Because there is a presence, and thus a potential difference, at every point in the flow, the same flow will replace the same amount of electrons in the orbital flows of each and every atom lined up along the flow.

The flow would also affect atoms in a plane at right angles to the flow, but would be divided among atoms thus positioned.

The point is, if we have a crystalline structure, such as the phosphorus on the head of a match, then a single flow of electrons will effect all of the atoms that it passes, replacing, to the extent of the flow, the electrons orbiting the nuclei of those atoms.

As a result, the flow of electrons has an affect far in excess of the potential difference of the flow itself.

What happens when the orbiting electrons are replaced by the flow's presence?

They themselves become flows!

Thus, in the example of the flow passing a row of atoms, as soon as the flow comes into existence, it creates ten thousand additional flows.

These ten thousand additional flows move through the structure, affecting ten thousand additional atoms, and in turn, each create ten thousand additional flows.

Now, in an instant, we have a hundred million flows.

It won't take too long before we have more flows than the structure can accommodate, and the flows will all be attempting to exit the crystalline surface at the same time.

Not being able to do so, the electrons that make them up start to back up at the crystalline surface. When the number of electrons wishing to exit becomes too great for the surface to hold them, they burst forth in the structured emissions we call light!

And, of course, they take the surface with them.

So, when we strike a match, the potential differences we create on the surface of the match head attract streams of electrons which create their own flows until so many flows are created that the phosphorus bursts into flame.

I have avoided the use of chain reaction. Chain reaction is used today to describe the field replacement of the units themselves from unstable boundary elements, elements that exist at the top level of the existing field.

However, understanding how field replacement leads

to ignition gives comprehension to the term.

Field replacement may or may not involve ignition and combustion. However, the cumulative process of field replacement created by the effect of the presence of a single flow of electrons on multiple atoms and molecules of atoms leads to ignition, and, as long as molecules of atoms and atoms are present that have orbiting electrons to emit as a result of the ignition, combustion will continue.

With ignition firmly in mind, we can see the field factual congruity by lighting one match, allowing it to establish an expanding sphere of light, and then moving the second match slowly into the sphere of light.

As the match moves into the stronger area of the first match's field, it begins to heat up, the result of field replacement allowing the electrons holding the atoms together to be emitted.

As the match is moved further into the field, the field replacement increases to the point that a number of atoms begin to release their orbiting clouds at the same time.

The match head eventually ignites and begins to combust. As long as the combustion process can replace the orbiting electrons of the match stem, the stem will continue the process of combustion, with the field replacement and ignition occurring in areas contiguous to the combustion process.

The concept of phlogiston was around long before Newton. The concept that what made up the matter was what the matter emitted was a good concept. It was only when matter was burdened with Newton's mass that we decided that what matter emitted had to be different from the matter itself.

In order to create a new theory of combustion, we had to get rid of everything about the old theory, even those areas of the old theory that the new theory didn't explain.

In the field factual congruity, instead of hunks of burning ice, a truly counterintuitive concept even when combustion is considered to be the combination of oxygen with combustible matter, comets can be viewed as matter that is undergoing combustion at an increasing rate the closer to the sun the comets travel.

This view is precluded by the concept of chemical combustion!

And, even though water does not combust, either in its creation, or in its dissolution, the concepts that explain combustion, explain ice.

Ice is water in crystalline form.

Water exists in a field in which the molecules that make it up are sufficiently stable to remain together under most environmental conditions. "Most environmental conditions" mean lying in sea level pools at temperatures between thirty two and two hundred and twelve degrees Fahrenheit.

Water does not have a strong molecular bond as is shown by the fact that we can move fairly smoothly through it, breaking the molecules apart as we go.

We have seen that combustion is the process of field replacement in which a massive flow of electrons massively replaces the electrons holding the atoms of the combustible matter together, with the electrons departing as light and the atoms breaking down into other atoms or molecules of atoms or recombining into other molecules.

The process of matter becoming cold is somewhat different.

If the highest potential difference is between an electron and the space around it, this alone provides a basis for the electron's motion. It is, itself, seeking to move toward a potential difference, and in the process moves.

Empty space might even be thought of as the ultimate potential difference, and perhaps it is that aspect of nothingness that causes electrons to come into existence in the first place.

In any event, the emptiness of space represents non activity, and non activity is certainly non heat, cold.

Thus, while the sun can be recognized as the ultimate in activity, or temperature, and light, the sun's emission field, as the diminishing activity produced by combustion, and thus gradient temperature from the hottest to the coldest, empty space is the coldest.

The sun's emissions provide a field in which water can exist in liquid form, say at forty degrees Fahrenheit.

What happens to a pool of water lying on the ground

when the sun goes down and the temperature drops to twenty degrees?

The water is made up of molecules of hydrogen and oxygen atoms held together by the potential differences of their nuclei, but spaced apart by the interference of the clouds of electrons in orbit around their nuclei.

When the sun goes down, there are going to be a lot of ambient electrons that were being used in inductive flows around the sun's emissions moving in the atmosphere.

The Earth containing the puddle is going to lose the stationary potential differences of the sun's emission field, and is therefore going to begin to attract the electrons out of the atmosphere. To be more precise, electrons in the atmosphere are going to move toward the excess potential difference that the setting sun has, by setting, created in the Earth.

The first electrons the potential difference of the Earth is going to affect are the electrons in the molecules of water. The Earth is going to attempt to draw electrons out of those molecules.

As long as there are plenty of electrons in the atmosphere, the water will serve as a conduit for electrons moving from the atmosphere into the Earth.

The movement, as long as it doesn't get out of hand, will keep the water warm. If the movement is too fast, it might start to break the molecules down into atoms right on the surface, where they would immediately recombine into surface mist, vapor, fog.

If there is a good cloud cover to capture the electrons close to the Earth, the water, and even the ground, might stay warm all night because of the movement.

But, sooner or later, the number of electrons in the atmosphere around the water will be depleted, and the potential difference of the Earth will begin to draw electrons out of the orbiting clouds of the atoms in the water molecules.

When one electron departs, and there is not another electron to take its place, what happens to the atoms in the water molecule?

The loss of an orbital electron has increased the potential difference of the nucleus losing the electron, and provided one less electron to interfere with the electrons orbiting other nuclei.

This causes the nuclei to move closer together.

When we examined molecules of water breaking down as a result of field replacement, we noted that the existence of the field replaces the potential differences between the nuclei, allowing the nuclei to drift apart.

Here, without the potential differences associated with field replacement, the potential differences between the nuclei increase as the process of losing electrons continues.

Before the structure started to lose electrons, it was in perfect balance, with all of the potential differences of the electrons used up in moving toward other potential differences or remaining stationary.

The opposing properties of the electrons are in equilibrium!

As the structure loses electrons, the potential differences of the nuclei are increasing, and the equilibrium of the structure is diminishing.

When we tried to construct a water molecule at sea level with an oxygen nucleus and a single hydrogen nucleus, we found that the result was not stable enough to remain together. An additional hydrogen nucleus was required to create stability.

Now that the structure is losing electrons from the orbital clouds of its atoms, the first nucleus to break out of the molecule is the last hydrogen nucleus in.

Free of the molecular structure, but still a part of it, the hydrogen nucleus begins to regain the orbiting electrons that it lost in the process of joining the molecule.

The oxygen atoms, in the meantime, are moving together as a result of their increasing potential differences, and, because in a physical structure, moving together also involves moving apart, pockets are formed into which the "last in" hydrogen nuclei move.

These hydrogen nuclei, with their orbital clouds, occupy more space than they did when they were combined with the oxygen atoms. The oxygen atoms, having moved closer together, occupy less space. The net result, however, is more space as a result of the increase in nuclei with orbital clouds.

The volume, and thus specific weight of the ice is less than the water that went into making it.

The reason that the ice forms so rapidly, and thus independent of the environment is because it is the separation of the hydrogen atoms from the oxygen atoms, and the resulting movement of the electrons from the orbital clouds of the oxygen atoms to the orbital clouds of the hydrogen atoms, that causes the final crystallization of the remaining molecules.

This is why the water/ice relationship is so unique.

The environment removes the electrons from the molecular structure causing the hydrogen nuclei to separate from the water molecules.

The hydrogen nuclei begin to remove electrons from the orbital clouds of the water molecules independent of the environment.

The rapid crystallization, initiated by the internal movement of electrons from the water molecules to the hydrogen nuclei, results in the final movement of the water molecule, now something less than one oxygen and two hydrogen nuclei, into a crystalline structure, a movement that replaces by far the largest number of orbiting electrons.

These electrons depart the structure as it becomes crystalline, and are measurable as heat.

What starts out as a process of electrons being

extracted from a molecular structure, then, results in the molecular structure, because of the internal relationship of the atoms that make it up, emitting heat into the environment as it crystallizes.

Water cools, and in a flash, forms ice, dumping massive amounts of heat into the environment as it snaps and crackles under the pressure of its physical expansion!

7   Electricity and Lightning

At this point, we have seen how water, or at least the atoms that make it up, enter the atmosphere. We've seen how water forms into ice.

In the process, we've seen the electron moving between and among potential differences.

Evaporation is a hazy concept that implies that when water disappears from the surface of bodies of water, it is saturating the atmosphere to various degrees. Actually, the molecules of water are breaking down into their respective atoms of hydrogen and oxygen, and in the process, they are removing heat from the environment.

When water forms into ice, it is adding large amounts of heat into the environment.

This, of course, means that when ice melts back into water, the process removes heat from the environment.

When the oxygen and hydrogen atoms get back together in an environment that will permit the existence of water, the process also cools the environment, removing heat from the atmosphere.

And, of course, to get back together, to reform into water molecules, there has to be heat, electrons, available in the environment.

It can be readily seen, then, that water is pretty central to the weather, outside of its appearance as snow, rain and ice.

The primary source of heat in the environment is the sun.

When the sun is up, the Earth gives up electrons into the environment, and the sun's emissions utilize those electrons in forming inductive flows.

When the sun goes down, the Earth is left with a potential difference toward which ambient electrons move.

Both the sun's rays and the Earth's surface are fixed.

It is the existence of large quantities of hydrogen and oxygen atoms that ameliorate what would otherwise be a fairly harsh result of the electron movements between these two sources.

We only have to look at the surface of the moon to see the results of the absence of hydrogen and oxygen.

Understanding the various relationships between oxygen and hydrogen, and the fields that produce those relationships, then, is basic to understanding the weather.

Along with the wind, they are the weather!

Lightning, the build up of ambient electrons in the environment, and their discharge by connecting potential differences within the environment, is a major result of the interaction of the available hydrogen and oxygen atoms with these ambient electrons in the environment.

The mechanics of lightning are considered to be unclear.

This is not surprising given the inability of modern

science to provide consistent pictures of physical phenomena, in this case, electricity.

Electricity is currently considered to be a flow of negative charges moving from positive to negative.

It is unfortunate that the non conductive view of electrical flow, with the electrons moving from negative to positive, isn't used because having the flow move from positive to negative hampers explanations of lightning.

This is because the only way to get a charge in the clouds under current concepts is to bounce pieces of ice against each other as they rise and descend in the cloud. This knocking about knocks electrons off the atoms of ice into the clouds, causing them to become negatively charged.

Having the negative charge in the clouds presents a serious problem, because it is obvious that the lightning doesn't come out of the ground and strike the clouds, it comes out of the clouds and strikes the ground.

But not to worry. Because like charges repel, it is clear that wherever the cloud roams, negative charges in the ground will be forced out. If negative charges are forced out, this leaves only positive charges in the ground.

These positive charges attract little feelers, streams of electrons that are tentatively breaching the insulation of the air shield, searching out opposite charges.

When one of the little feelers hits an upraised golf club, it triggers an opposite flow of positive charges, a flow of colossal proportions that fries the golfer on the spot.

Well, they might not be positive charges, perhaps the circuit just closed and they're a continuation of negative charges.

Hmmm.

Perhaps electricity just comes into existence when the circuit is completed.

Circuit? No wonder we have the electricity moving as if it were in a conductor.

We're in domain problems here, again, but the name of the game is to get out of Rome, which is what we'll quickly do.

I can't help but point out in passing that the imposition of mathematically precise positive and negative quantities for electricity locks the mind into conceptual explanations for lightning that not only don't explain, but sow total confusion.

To understand what creates lightning, it's necessary to sidestep the cornswoggle that is used when the description of lightning is grafted onto unclear concepts of electricity, and produce a clear description of electricity, which if it approximates reality, will provide us with a startling clear picture of lightning!

When we produce electricity, we are concentrating the electrons that make up electromagnetic flows so that the resulting electrical flows can do physical work for us.

One of my favorite rooms contains a generator.

A generator distills electricity out of the ambient environment with the use of magnets or electromagnetic fields.

We started out describing magnets as matter whose atomic structure requires that the nuclei share orbits in a manner that results in electrons externally orbiting the structure.

Electrons flow into one end of the magnet and pass the atoms held in place by their shared potential differences. We saw this principle when we lined up atoms and allowed a stream to pass all of the atoms, replacing orbiting electrons in each atom equally.

With magnetic material, the crystalline structure of the atoms prohibits orbiting electrons to balance the structure, and the only way the structure can obtain equilibrium is to capture ambient electrons out of the environment and put them in a shared orbit that results in a part of the orbit being external to the structure.

Thus, the electrons pass through the magnet, out one end, and then move around to re-enter the magnet at the other end.

If we move a conductor parallel to the flow, we will cause some of the electrons in the magnetic lines of force to flow into the conductor.

We can accomplish the same thing by creating a flow of electrons in a conductor. The flow will create an inductive flow at right angles to the conductor. If we move a conductor parallel to this flow, we will cause some of the electrons in the inductive flows to flow into the conductor.

In either case, the electrons that are diverted from the inductive flows into the conductor begin to move within the physical confines of the conductor as a result of their property of motion.

The definition of a conductor is a crystalline structure whose atoms are positioned in equilibrium with minimal orbital clouds. The current definition of the conductor as atomically porous is appropriately descriptive, so long as porous isn't considered to be the God-awful holes that have been featured in explanations of electricity since the invention of the transistor.

The motion of the electrons in the conductor is guided by the potential differences between the nuclei of the atoms that make up the conductor.

Marginally orbiting electrons in the conductor immediately join the electrons being tipped into the conductor, which causes a start up surge of electricity when the flow is first established.

With a minimum of orbital electrons obstructing the flow, the electrons tipped into the conductor by its movement parallel with the magnetic lines of force or inductive flows of electrons are free to move in accordance with their property of motion within the conductor.

However, in order to move within the conductor, they

have to have some place to move to within the conductor.

The only place that they can move to is a potential difference. A potential difference is found where there is a deficit of electrons.

There is deficit of electrons at the point in the conductor at which the conductor is removing electrons from the electron flow!

Thus, if the conductor is hooked up to itself, put in a closed circuit, then the electrons will return to the point in the conductor that they entered.

If we put a load, such as a light, on the conductor, then the electrons will create field replacement in the load.

The load is made up of a filament of atoms with orbital clouds so that when the flow of electricity reaches the load, field replacement will cause the orbital clouds to be emitted as light.

The atoms of the filament, however, create a reverse field replacement on the flow once the flow has replaced their orbital clouds.

Once the atoms of the filament begin to emit the structured light, they attract the electrons in the electrical flow to replace the electrons that have been emitted as light.

These electrons in turn are emitted as light.

The load, the light filament, thus becomes a continuous potential difference in the circuit.

The electrons tipped into the conductor head directly for the potential difference, the load, the light, where they are immediately put to use in forming the portion of the electromagnetic spectrum, light, dictated by the rate of combustion.

The electrons that make up the flow are being tipped into the flow by moving the conductor through magnetic lines of force or inductive flows.

The electrons that make up these magnetic lines of force or inductive flows are present because of the potential differences that create the magnetic lines of force or inductive flows.

When electrons are tipped into the conductor from the magnetic lines of force or inductive flows, they have to be replaced by ambient electrons from the environment.

A generator room is a fascinating place because it demonstrates the second circuit.

The light being emitted from the filament is made up of electrons that are expanding in all directions, an expanding sphere.

The surface of the sphere of light expands and as it does so, it diminishes until it reaches the six sides of the room. It then begins to bounce back and forth in ever expanding spheres of light until the light breaks down into the individual electrons that make it up.

These individual electrons become ambient electrons in the environment, available for recycling into the flows that are feeding electrons into the conductor.

The second circuit of electron flow in the generator room, then, is from the ambient field into the magnetic lines of force or inductive flows, then into the conductor, then into the load, then into the expanding light and finally back into the ambient field where they are once again available to recycle into the magnetic lines of force or inductive flows.

If our room has a huge generator that feeds electricity to cities hundreds of miles away, then it might need a non apparent source of electrons to feed the generators.

This inexhaustible source is the emissions from the receding ball of fire which is located some fifty to a hundred miles beneath the concrete floor on which the generator is sitting.

When we produce electricity, we are distilling ambient electrons out of the environment and concentrating them in usable flows.

Another phrase that describes the process is to harvest ambient electrons.

The second way that we make electricity is chemically, and to demonstrate this it is best to go out into deep space where we can build idealistic examples in the laboratories of our minds.

The nice thing about elements is diversity. When the atom with the greatest number of units in its nucleus broke down, it could only break down into atoms that had less than that number of units in the nucleus.

If this heaviest atom has four hundred units in its nucleus, then there can only be four hundred possible elements.

However, when elements begin to combine chemically so that they become compounds of elements, the number of resulting possible compounds is endless.

Each of the resulting combinations of elements has a potential difference with respect to the environment, and more importantly, with respect to each other.

If we take two of the combinations of elements with a potential difference between them, and connect them with a conductor, electrons from the orbiting clouds of the atoms with the lesser potential difference with respect to the environment will flow to and become a part of the orbital clouds of the atoms with a greater potential difference with respect to the environment.

We don't need a circuit for this to occur, and in fact we separate the two compounds by a non conductor, a switch that we place on the connecting conductor to turn the electron flow on and off.

A flashlight illustrates this arrangement, with the "positive" and "negative" ends of the battery being the two compounds, the light bulb, the detector telling us when there is a flow, and the on/off switch being the non conductor placed across the conductor.

Instead of a flashlight battery, we are going to use two

compounds with different potential differences. We'll use a conductor, but instead of a switch, we'll use a rheostat, which will allow us to turn the conductor itself into the detector, saving on parts.

We could take the compounds out of any battery, but let's use compound "A" and compound "B". Compound "B" has a greater potential difference with respect to the space around it than compound "A". We'll put compound "A" on the left and compound "B" on the right.

If we use our conductor to connect the two compounds, we would establish a flow of electrons that would move from left to right, "A" to "B".

But we're not too bright, or maybe we have a shortage of materials in our mental laboratory, and we hook up a conductor that is way to small for the difference in potential that exists between the two compounds. We can't allow the full flow to pass through the wire because it would destroy the wire.

Thus, we hook up our rheostat on the conductor.

The rheostat works like a switch. When it is closed, the conductor is broken so that there can be no flow between compound "A" and compound "B". If we turn the knob on the rheostat just a little, just a little flow will pass through the conductor. Turn the knob a lot, and a lot of current will flow through the conductor.

If we open the rheostat just enough to allow one electron at a time to pass through, then the potential difference of compound "B" will attract a flow of single electrons from compound "A".

What we have done by connecting the two compounds is to alter the potential difference of each with the space around it.

The electrons will flow until the two compounds together reach a balance with the field.

If there were ambient electrons available to compound "B", they would move to compound "B" along with orbiting electrons from compound "A". Compound "A"'s orbiting electrons would also re-enter the field as ambient electrons. This is why the compounds in a battery have to be insulated from the surrounding field.

One other effect of the field can be noted. If the field is fifty below zero, there are no ambient electrons (the definition of heat) in the field. The field itself acts as a conductor, pulling electrons out of the compounds until there is no potential difference between them, and none available to flow if there were a potential difference between them.

The car battery won't start!

Once we have a single flow of electrons moving through the conductor, we can note that the electrons can move through the conductor because the conductor is a crystalline structure whose atoms are held together by mutual potential differences among chains of nuclei. There are only a minimal amount of electrons in orbital clouds and these electrons will become a part of the flow as the flow increases until an optimum level is reached. As we shall see, the optimum level is the level at which the electron flow does not interfere with the physical structure of the conductor.

The single flow of electrons passes easily through the conductor without affecting its internal structure.

Normally, the flow would establish an inductive flow. Insulation prevents this from occurring, and because our laboratory is in imaginary space where there are no electrons available to form inductive flows, we can focus totally on the primary electrical flow.

If we bump the flow up from a single flow of electrons, we can reach the level at which an optimum flow can move through the crystalline structure without affecting the potential differences between the nuclei of the atoms.

If we add one more flow to this flow, then we are going to begin replacing the potential differences in the nuclei of the atoms that make up the conductor.

We noted at the outset that the conductor wasn't sufficient to handle the full flow of electrons that would be established by connecting the two compounds without the rheostat.

By opening the rheostat past the point at which the conductor can accommodate the flows, we are allowing the flows to replace the potential differences that are holding the nuclei of the atoms in the conductor together.

The conductor will start to behave like the filament in the light bulb.

It will begin to emit electrons.

So increasing the flow of electrons past the conductor's ability to direct them to the potential difference of compound "B" will result in their emission from the conductor, which, of course, is measurable as heat.

Now, we are going to become really devil may care, and turn the rheostat slowly upward.

As we do so, the number of electrons in the flow increases, the number of electrons converted by the conductor into heat increases, and before we know it, the potential differences between the nuclei that make up the conductor will be replaced.

The crystalline structure begins to break down. The conductor begins to melt.

But we aren't finished.

We jam the rheostat one final turn, sending the full jolt of electricity through the undersized conductor.

So many electrons are released at the same time that they can't all leave the area.

They line up until the melting surface of the conductor can no longer hold them.

They burst forth in a flash of light, reducing the conductor to its constituent atoms in the process.

And, if there's oxygen around, there might be some ash left!

Lightning is the massive movement of electrons between potential differences in the environment.

To understand lightning, it is only necessary to analogize it to the movement of electrons between the two compounds.

The movement of electrons between the two compounds occurs because one of the compounds has an excess of electrons when compared to the other compound.

All we have to determine is where, in the environment, such disbalances occur, and see if lightning results.

We could check ourselves by ensuring that the lightning actually moved from an area with a relative excess of electrons to an area with a relative deficit of electrons.

One type of lightning, known as heat lightning, doesn't provide such a check, but should be mentioned as a baseline.

Our definition of heat is excess electrons in the environment, what we have described as ambient electrons in an ambient field.

If the atmosphere is dry, with few hydrogen and oxygen atoms, and thus no clouds, when the sun goes down, liberating the electrons that were being used as inductive flows by the sun's rays, the Earth is going to have a deficit of electrons with respect to the ambient electrons in the atmosphere.

The ambient electrons are going to be attracted to the Earth's surface, but there are no ready paths for them to enter the Earth.

In the morning, when the sun comes up, the trees and plants, grass and flowers provide a path for the electrons to move from the Earth to the atmosphere. However, trees and plants don't grow out of the sky because the medium is not stable enough to support roots. By the very nature of things, the relationship between the Earth and the atmosphere does not permit the ready transfer of these ambient electrons back into the Earth. In fact, the trees and plants and other morning paths actually close up to protect themselves from what would be fiber destroying flows back in the first path available.

Thus, the potential difference between the Earth and the atmosphere builds up, with the Earth having massive deficits of electrons. In addition, the potential differences within the atmosphere build up as more electrons than can be absorbed occupy particular areas.

If there are no clouds, these electrons will build up to the point that they will displace the orbiting clouds in the molecules of air, resulting in the discharges we see as heat lightning, the heat of course being the result of the superabundance of electron buildup.

This situation provides a good view of what is happening with ambient electrons

Ambient electrons can dictate their own environment. Atoms of nitrogen, oxygen and hydrogen will exist independently of each other if there is a build up of ambient electrons, which is heat.

In addition, the potential differences inherent in an area with a high ambient electron population increases.

Thus, an atom of hydrogen would be affected in two ways. If there was no field, and no ambient electrons, the hydrogen atom would have the largest orbiting cloud of electrons possible. However, as the field increases, or as the ambient electrons in the field increase, field replacement reduces the number of electrons needed in the orbiting cloud to balance the potential difference of the nucleus.

The ambient electrons also work as a field to replace potential difference in a nucleus.

The result of the field replacement, then, is the reduction of electrons in the orbital clouds. The nuclei of atoms can therefore exist in closer proximity!

This means that more hydrogen atoms can occupy a given area.

The next effect of the ambient field is to counter the effect of the attractive force on the atom.

Normally, the weight of the nitrogen and oxygen atoms would force the hydrogen atoms to rise. However, when the orbital clouds of the hydrogen atoms have been replaced by the electrons in the ambient field, the hydrogen atoms become embedded in the ambient field.

The ambient electrons are hugging the surface of the Earth because of the Earth's potential difference. The hydrogen atoms are embedded in the ambient field.

The hydrogen atoms remain close to the surface of the Earth!

What holds true for the hydrogen atoms also applies to the oxygen atoms.

As the ambient field increases, the oxygen nuclei's orbiting clouds are reduced, the number of oxygen nuclei that can occupy a given area increases, and the nuclei stay embedded in the field along with the hydrogen nuclei.

This is why water does not evaporate and condense as water molecules.

Water molecules break down into their constituent atoms in sunlight, or as a result of ambient electrons in the environment, and reform as the ambient electrons are removed from the field.

The more ambient electrons there are in the environment, the greater the number of oxygen and hydrogen atoms per volume the environment will be able to hold embedded in it.

This is humidity, with the water molecules available for break down in the environment determining the relative humidity.

In short, the warmer the air, the more makings of water

it can hold!

However, this is not the weather, the storm systems that are generated at the equator and work themselves north.

Humidity is basically a local condition, and when environmental conditions change so as to permit a loss of electrons, the atoms of oxygen and hydrogen reform into water molecules and precipitate out of the atmosphere.

The cloud systems that originate as a result of the equatorial breakdown of water molecules provide a magnet for ambient electrons because of the ice flecks, crystals of hydrogen and oxygen nuclei, that make them up.

How these ice flecks are formed is discussed at the end of Chapter Eight.

When ice forms, it gives up heat. When it melts, it takes in large quantities of electrons, which, again, is heat.

Lightning is the by product of the ice flecks that make up the clouds mixing with air masses filled with ambient electrons.

As the cloud mixes with the warmer air, the potential differences of the ice flecks attracts electrons out of the warm air mass, forming water molecules in the process.

The cloud becomes a magnet for ambient electrons in the environment.

As the cloud converts the ice flecks into water

molecules, the excessive build up of electrons is discharged as lightning into areas with deficits of electrons.

The cloud becomes a sort of pulse generator driven by the available electrons and the potential differences of the ice flecks, and stationary potential differences in the Earth.

A single cloud can become a source of repeated discharges. The lightning depletes the cloud of the electrons needed to convert the ice flecks into water, and the potential differences of the ice flecks again attract massive numbers of ambient electrons out of the environment.

The process continues to repeat itself until the ambient electrons in the immediate area of the cloud are depleted, or the ice that makes up the cloud has turned to water and fallen to the ground.

Witness, for example, an ominous storm cloud moving across the sunny Earth.

As it moves, it blocks out the sun.

Large numbers of ambient electrons are liberated into the area beneath the cloud as the sun's rays are blocked by the cloud.

At the same time, the departure of the sun's rays creates a potential difference in the Earth beneath the cloud, an area where, as a result, there is a massive deficit of electrons.

In a process that will be described in Chapter Nine, the cloud is continuously converting ice crystals that are dropping from its uppermost regions into water molecules in the lower regions.

The process of converting ice to water attracts the ambient electrons freshly liberated into the atmosphere.

They flock to the cloud and are immediately attracted toward the potential difference in the Earth.

The first spark of lightning gives birth to a second spark, and a third and a fourth.

As the cloud marches across the Earth, it is a veritable dynamo. It blocks the sun, liberating the electrons from inductive flows and creating a deficit of electrons in the Earth. It harvests the ambient electrons liberated from the inductive flows, concentrates them, and zaps them into the electron needy earth below. When the cloud departs, the sun's rays once again liberate the electrons from the Earth, and employ them in establishing inductive flows.

Instead of exhausting the ambient electrons in the atmosphere, the cloud is generating its own ambient electrons as it sails across the fruited plain, harvesting electrons in the process of converting itself from ice to water, converting the electrons to lightning, pummeling the Earth with the lightning, and then moving on, treating the quiet countryside in its path to a symphony of sound and light in its presence, and leaving wonder in its wake.

Incredible!

Marvelous!

Elegant.

8   The Wind

You just don't get no respect from modern science unless you are able to mathematise your concepts!

The fact that concepts cannot be mathematised, and that mathematization has therefore resulted in modern science, hands down the most distorted picture of physical reality ever devised, does not much change the situation.

Weather starts at the equator and moves up in a northeasterly direction.

Just like the orbiting of the planets, which appear to repetitively end up at the end of the year where they started at the beginning of the year, at least when they are measured in relation to one another, the jet stream and the weather move from west to east.

The most difficult thing to remember is that when the north wind blows it will freeze your nose and even assigning the direction the wind blows as the direction from which the wind blows is manmade.

No idiocy we can make up, no pretensions that our mathematical conceptualizations have anything at all to do with reality, will change that reality.

The idea with weather is that high pressure should move the atmosphere to low pressure.

We have seen that high pressure is not more air piled up. It's just more units of atoms per volume of air.

It is relative.

"Heavier" air does move into areas of less heavy air. This is both conceptually and physically valid.

Thus, when we look at air at the north pole, air which is chilled to the max, we see atoms whose nuclei have been robbed of orbiting electrons and therefore whose nuclei have increased potential differences that cause them to move closer together, air which, as a result, has more units per volume than the warmer air to the south.

It is only logical that this heavier cold air should push into the warmer air in a series of steps that eventually result in its moving all the way to the equator.

If this is true, and it is fairly well measurable, then the surface wind should blow south and the jet stream should blow north.

It doesn't, so what makes the south wind blow from west to east, the north wind blow from east to west and weather move from southwest to northeast?

Well, if you shoot a rocket off due north at the equator, in the direction the south winds should blow, its path will describe an arc to the right, because by the time it lands, the Earth will have moved to the right.

And if you shoot the rocket off from the north pole toward the equator, its path will still describe an arc to the right, this because the Earth has moved to the right.

I noted that the right hand rule applied to the Earth as well as inductance. Take your right hand and hold the thumb up. The fingers will curl in the direction of the Earth's rotation. Shoot a rocket off from the tip of your little finger while you are closing your fingers. As it lands on your index finger, it will have described an arc to the right.

The rocket might have slowed down a little because of air resistance, and people that are in the business of shooting off rockets, I think they are called rocket scientists, have to adjust their telemetry for this effect, but the rocket has the speed of the Earth's rotation when it takes off, and this speed is maintained.

That's why its flight describes an arc.

It's not something, however, that can be used to mathematise the weather!

The rocket moved in a straight line. We, as observers independent of the Earth's rotation, are the ones that created the curve.

The desire to mathematise has as its basis the desire to awe the populace by predicting events. Modern science predicting where Venus will be in the year two million, three thousand, eight hundred and ninety nine isn't much different than the shaman atop the parapet flinging his arm out into the future at the exact moment the moon moves in front of the sun darkening the cowed populace into maintaining its excessive level of tax payments.

Making predictions, unless it is about something like how much stress an airplane wing will take, is a rather useless occupation.

Because predicting the weather can be very profitable, however, its always nice if we can delude ourselves, and our potential customers, into thinking that we can.

And the best way to do that is to come up with some mathematical hocus pocus that will get scientific recognition.

The Coriolis effect, or force if you're really forceful, is such an accomplishment.

The explanation starts out by shooting the rocket from the north pole. It lands at a point to the west of the point that it would have landed had the Earth not been turning.

The arc that appears as a result of the time lapse resulting from the rocket's flight is in the direction of the easterly trade winds, the winds in the lower atmosphere that blow to the west.

Because the rocket is being shot off from the north pole, it has no easterly momentum.

However, the rocket is still moving in a straight line and we, as independent observers are using our perception of the passage of time and the rotation of the planet to describe the arc to the right.

Thus, as physics books will tell you, the Coriolis effect is an effect not a force, an illusion that results from changing relationships, not something that can change those relationships!

The rocket's path is not curved.   The curve is a representation, rather than the result of a force.

But weather, like psychoanalysis, badly needs objective mathematization to gain acceptance as a science.

Thus, the cornswoggle goes something like this:

If the rocket's path were the result of a force, then the force would work to turn the wind to the west, just like the rocket turns to the west.

As we know for a fact that the wind is moving to the west, it must be moving as a result of a force.

Sir Isaac Newton, the greatest scientific mind that has ever existed proved that there cannot be a reaction without an opposite action.

Therefore, the Coriolis effect is a force.

Otherwise, the wind wouldn't blow to the west!

Thus is the Coriolis effect, a result of perception, mathematised.

As winds flow north, the Coriolis effect causes them to move in an easterly direction, or to the right.   The mathematised force is mathematised in conjunction with the mathematised isobaric pressure and we end up with mathematically predictable weather, or in the terms of the textbooks, a description of reality that so matches reality that it must be a correct description of reality!

Newton's laws of motion are also said to provide an exact description of reality, the movement of the planets in the solar system, just as the moon, together with the sun is said to provide the vehicle for predicting the tides.

The fact of the matter is, the moon's orbit is so unstable, and therefore so unpredictable, that it took a ton of volunteers to find out where it would be when we sent our astronauts there. And they didn't find out by feeding figures into computers. They did so by taking constant physical measurements of where it was. The Earth's spin increases and decreases, the Earth and the moon speed up and slow down, the planetary orbits are so chaotic as to spawn a new science that says that when systems become chaotic, they become stable.

As far as the being able to predict the tides by reference to the moon, forget it. It can't be done.

These are cases in which we have measured reality, and then come up with some sort of mathematical construct which approximates that reality.

It wouldn't be so bad, except that we have to use concepts to think, and when we have mathematical systems that approximate reality, we think they validate our concepts.

Concepts are ideas. Ideas are not provable. If we have an idea that objects of unlike weight fall at the same rate, and we drop two unlike objects, and they drop at the same rate, then we haven't got an idea, we have a fact.

If we say that the objects fall because gravity is a property of mass, and then prove that the moon falls at the same rate that a rock falls, we haven't proven the idea.

We still have an idea! The rate at which two objects fall has nothing to do with what make them fall.

The Coriolis effect is the result of tracing the trajectory of a projectile moving between two points on a rotating sphere in two different situations, from the equator where the projectile has the momentum of the rotating sphere, and from the north pole where the projectile doesn't have the momentum of the rotating sphere.

The arc of the rocket's perceived course travels right in both cases for different reasons, so even the effect is not uniform.

To think of the wind as something that lifts off the ground, and as it moves north curves east, causing it to move with respect to the air that hasn't lifted off the ground and traveled north, is, to put it mildly, to be confused.

A nonexistent force does not cause the jet streams!

When I state that we cannot mathematise concepts, I don't mean to say that we are free to devise concepts that work outside of the mathematical limitations of reality.

There are certain facts that we live with, and any explanation for those facts must be in accord with the mathematical measurements associated with those facts.

Thus, if we were standing on the geographical north pole, the pole determined by the axis of the Earth's rotation, we could say that we would be spinning around a total of one turn every twenty four hours.

We are, in essence, not experiencing any forward motion with respect to the Earth's rotation.

On the other hand, if we are standing on the equator, we know that we are experiencing forward motion with respect to the Earth's rotation.

We are moving at about a thousand miles an hour, and making a complete revolution of about twenty five thousand miles each twenty four hour period.

These are the mathematical facts that we can neither dispute nor ignore.

Any explanation of what goes on with respect to the atmosphere has to take these mathematical facts into consideration.

We are not mathematising our concepts into some coherent, internally consistent system, and then bending all of reality to those controlling concepts.

We are measuring reality, and asking, what is going to happen within the confines of that reality!

If we come up with what is actually happening, then we have provided a consistent picture of physical phenomena, rather than fitting physical phenomena into our consistent picture.

When we stand on the equator, we are not blown off of our feet.

Because we know that we are moving at a thousand

miles an hour, and we are not being blown off of our feet, we are darn sure that the air that would blow us off our feet is moving as fast as we are.

Thus, we know that the air at the equator is moving at about a thousand miles an hour.

This isn't something like Newton's proposition that an object will travel in a straight line unless a force acts on the object to keep it from traveling in a straight line.

Even though all reasonable men can agree that this is a correct statement, the fact is, objects don't travel in straight lines unless something is making them travel in straight lines.

Objects don't travel unless a force makes them travel!

That's why our picture of the universe is backward. We assume motion and only examine what might be slowing motion down instead of living in the real world, where objects come to rest with respect to existing forces, and then ask of objects that keep moving, what is making them move?

The application of this silliness becomes especially absurd when it is molecules of air that are supposed to be in perpetual motion!

We are not starting out with something that doesn't exist, an object traveling in a straight line.

We are starting out with facts that do exist, the fact that the Earth is a sphere, its equator is the largest diameter of the sphere that a point on the sphere's axis can describe, and that when the sphere is rotating, the point on the equator is moving at a rate that covers the distance of the equator in the time of the rotation.

We can't escape this.

It exists!

Now, if we are standing on the north geographical pole, we are stationary with respect to the Earth's rotation.

And, as we stand there spinning, we are not being blown anywhere.

This means that the air at the north geographic pole is not traveling at a thousand miles an hour.

It is not traveling at all.

It is motionless.

If the air at the north pole is not moving, and the air at the equator is moving at a thousand miles an hour, then we know that air moving from the north pole to the equator is going to have to speed up from nothing to one thousand miles an hour by the time it reaches the equator.

And, if the air at the equator is moving at a thousand miles an hour, and the air at the north pole is not moving, then we know that air moving from the equator to the north pole is going to have to slow down from a thousand miles an hour to nothing by the time it reaches the north pole.

And therein lie the winds!

The weather maps that I generally look at are generated from satellites that cover North America. Because weather is a product of cold air masses moving from the poles to the equator, rising and moving back to the poles, looking at the weather patterns over the U.S. will tell us what is happening everywhere. The only local variation will be the result of geographical differences.

Weather comes out of the southwest pacific and the Gulf of Mexico and moves in a generally northeast direction. Storm systems form and move east or northeast.

We don't have storms forming in the northeast and moving west. We don't have weather moving from north to south. The jet stream drops south in the winter and causes havoc with the storm systems moving from west to east, but this is a result of the shift of the pressure-gradient force resulting from the sun's ecliptic plane, the point on the Earth at which the sun is directly overhead, moving south. As the thermal equator moves south, the cold Arctic air drops with it.

This northeastward movement is mathematised as the northward moving wind turning east as a result of the Coriolis force.

It is actually the wind failing to slow down sufficiently to match the speed of the Earth's surface as the air is pushed north by the displacement of the pressure-gradient force!

A given volume of air mass at the equator will have less weight than the same quantity of air to the north because the air mass to the north is cooler.

Weight is the equivalent of air pressure, with the more atoms of air per volume, the heavier the air.

The warmer the air, the less atoms there are per volume because the field which produces the temperature replaces the mutual potential differences of the atoms allowing them to move apart.

As noted, when atoms of air move apart in warm weather, space is created for additional hydrogen and oxygen atoms if they are available in the environment through the breakdown of water molecules.

The addition of these atoms from the breakdown of water molecules makes the air heavier.

The cold air, however, will always push warm air up because if the warm air becomes heavy enough to sink into the cold air, the cold air will remove electrons, heat, from the warm air, which will cause the hydrogen and oxygen atoms to reform into water molecules, rain (the same as reaching the dew point, which also generates heat).

As the air at the equator rises, its weight, here a result of vertical pressure, begins to cause it to spread physically over the available area.

The available area is on the top of the incoming cooler air mass, and the equatorial air mass cascades over the top of the incoming air and begins its journey north.

The air begins this journey at a speed of about one thousand miles an hour.

As it tumbles over onto the incoming air, then, it is moving at a thousand miles per hour.

This is the air's momentum.

Its momentum is derived from its proximity to the rotating surface of the Earth. The further away from the surface of the Earth the air, the less effect that surface has on it. The surface has a major effect up to five hundred feet.

The cold air starts out at the north pole with no momentum. As it moves south, it is speeding up, but it is not moving as fast as the Earth itself, because the diameter of the Earth is always increasing as the wind moves south.

This results in the trade winds, with the air appearing to move in a westward direction.

If I am standing facing east, I am facing the direction that I am traveling, along with the surface of the Earth, at about eight hundred miles an hour. To the north, the Earth is traveling less than eight hundred miles an hour, while to the south, the Earth is traveling faster than eight hundred miles an hour.

Even if the southward moving air had speeded up to the speed of the Earth just to my north, it would still be going ten miles an hour less than I am going by the time that it dropped to my position.

As a result, it would appear to be blowing in my face, when in fact I am just moving faster than the speed to which it has been accelerated.

Of course, as it reaches my face, and partially as a result of hitting me in the face, it is accelerating so that by the time it moves ten miles to the south, it might have speeded up to my speed, although it wouldn't be moving as fast as someone standing ten miles to the south would be moving!

As the air moves from the north pole to the equator in response to the pressure-gradient force, it has to speed up to one thousand miles an hour.

All things being equal, the southward moving air at any point in its journey is speeding up, but at any point it has not reached the speed that the surface of the planet is traveling at that point.

Thus, because the point on the surface of the planet is moving west to east, the air appears to be moving east to west, even though the air is accelerating in a west to east direction!

The southward moving air mass is not bringing weather with it because it is composed of cold air which is compressed, and therefore has no room for the hydrogen and oxygen atoms whose conversion to water molecules makes the weather.

The effect of this air mass on the weather is twofold.

It is a high pressure area around which the lower, lighter, northward moving air masses have to move.

To the extent that the southward moving air maintains its cohesiveness, it breaks up the weather.

Second, as noted, it is available to intermingle with the northward moving air which is laden with the atoms of oxygen and hydrogen that can form into water molecules to create the weather.

If we put various points on a meridian between the equator and the north pole, we will have points that are traveling at different rates of speed because as we go north, the diameters of the circles that make up the paths we are traveling decrease, although every point on the meridian makes one rotation in the same time period, every twenty four hours.

This means that any point on the surface of the Earth north of the equator is going slower than the point to the south of it.

Because the northward moving air masses are moving at least as fast as they were moving when they passed the last point on the meridian, they are always going faster than the point on the planet directly beneath them.

The northward moving air masses have the additional problem of traveling over air masses rather than over physical geography. As a result, friction does not play a big factor in slowing them down to the Earth's speed.

The result are bands of eastward moving air, the jet streams that appear in specific geographical locations as the seasons change.

The effect of the jet stream air separating itself from the interactions of the lower air masses can be seen by drawing a quarter of a circle to represent the arc from the north pole to the equator and then drawing a vertical line north from the equator.

The air at the top of the northward moving air masses is the air occupying the greatest volume and thus having the fewest molecules. It is air that has had the oxygen and hydrogen atoms separated out from it, air without clouds.

As the northward moving air reaches thirty degrees latitude, it has to drop to meet the curvature of the Earth. This occurs again at approximately sixty degrees latitude. To see this, it is merely necessary to adjust the northward moving arrow by thirty degrees.

Because the air north of the jet streams drops, forcing weather producing clouds into the southward moving air masses, the thirty and sixty degree curvature points also affect the weather to their south, providing the areas with abundant precipitation.

Temperature differentials determine where these jet streams exist. When the northern hemisphere is tilted toward the sun in its summer months, the jet streams move north, because the corresponding temperature differentials move north. When the northern hemisphere is tilted away from the sun in winter, the jet streams migrate south.

The jet stream does not move south dragging cold air behind it. It moves south with the sun's ecliptic plane, which changes the thirty and sixty degree lines on the physical Earth as the seasons change!

The air that is moving north, however, is still moving as fast as it was when it started its journey.

The air masses, then, as they travel north, are always going faster than the surface of the Earth beneath it.

This is so even though they are beginning to slow down as they travel north as a result of the friction encountered with the heavier, slower moving lower air masses.

Thus, even though at the latitude that I am writing this, the surface of the Earth is moving at about eight hundred miles an hour, the upper atmosphere is moving at anywhere from eighty to one hundred and fifty miles an hour faster.

The reason that the weather moves generally from southwest to northeast is because it is moving east as a result of its initial equatorial velocity, while it is moving north as a result of its displacement by the pressure-gradient force.

The air, then, all things being equal, is moving at three speeds, the lower, southward moving air mass accelerating at a rate that lags the speed of the Earth's surface, the cloud filled layer slowing down, but still moving faster than the speed of the Earth's surface and the upper thin air failing to slow, and thus racing ahead of the speed of the Earth's surface.

At first glance, we would make the assumption that as the air masses moved north, the air with the most atoms per volume would sink, causing the air with the least atoms per volume to rise.

However, because the air has momentum, the effect of weight is reversed.

When I refer to momentum, I am not referring to Newton's fantasy of acceleration imbuing an object with a property that tends to keep it in motion.

I'm just noting the reality that it's going to take whatever it took to get an object moving to get it to stop.

This isn't too sophisticated a concept. It takes forever to get an oil tanker up to full speed, but once it gets there, you better know where your going, because it's going to take forever for it to stop.

If we take a bucket of oxygen and nitrogen atoms, and sit them on the north pole, the oxygen atoms are going to sink to the bottom of the bucket (or, to be technical, the nitrogen atoms are going to rise to the top).

The same thing is going to happen on the equator when the air masses containing oxygen and nitrogen atoms are moving at one thousand miles an hour. The oxygen atoms are still heavier than the nitrogen atoms.

When the air masses begin to slow down, however, the effect of weight reverses itself.

The atoms with the most units tied together in their nuclei, the heaviest atoms, are going to be the atoms that are the last to slow down!

When the water molecule breaks down at the equator, the resulting atoms take in electrons. This process of "evaporation" removes electrons from the ambient field. There is, therefore, no ambient field of electrons in which the hydrogen atom can embed itself.

As a result, the hydrogen atoms are separated from the oxygen atoms.

Without this process, we would have no equatorial clouds to move north. If the hydrogen atoms stayed embedded in the equatorial field with the oxygen atoms, they would just "condense" back into water molecules when the sun went down.

With the hydrogen atoms separated from the oxygen atoms, the hydrogen atoms move into the upper reaches of the air mass.

Because the inverse square law determines area, the higher the air mass rises, the greater the area is into which it moves.

Just as with air pressure, which involves the number of atoms per volume, with the ambient field, the greater the volume available for a given number of ambient electrons, the less the ambient field.

This means that the higher the air mass goes, the less the ambient field is, and thus the cooler it is.

As the hydrogen atoms rise, the potential difference between their nuclei and the field increases.

With a lessening ambient field, the increasing potential

difference of the nuclei cause them to attract each other.

The oxygen atoms, meanwhile, are being pushed up and north with the air mass. As the air mass travels north, it begins to slow down.

As the air mass slows down, the nitrogen atoms are the first to slow down, with the oxygen atoms being the last to slow down.

The process of slowing down, therefore, differentiates the air mass so that the oxygen atoms are at the top of the air mass rather than at the bottom where they normally would be without the slowing process.

The top of the air mass is precisely where the hydrogen atoms are, and, as the potential differences of the oxygen nuclei with the field have increased, the oxygen and hydrogen nuclei come together in structures that are not ice as it is seen as a result of freezing, but ice flecks, molecules of hydrogen and oxygen formed together from the potential differences of the individual hydrogen and oxygen nuclei.

In short, clouds!

9   The Rain

We now have the makings of rain, the clouds which will produce the rain, the weather, moving north with the wind.

Looking at the United States, the weather follows one or more of several established patterns.

Weather moves in vortical weather systems or in weather systems organized as fronts.

Vortical weather systems involve air masses that move in a counterclockwise direction. If you put the base of your right hand over the U.S. and point your thumb up, your fingers will be curling in the direction these vortical air masses move.

Vortical weather systems form in the Pacific Ocean west of the U.S., over the U.S. and in the Atlantic Ocean southeast of the U.S. They are the result of weather systems moving north on the east side of descending, high pressure air masses.

Because the Pacific Ocean is so vast, northeastward moving air masses can travel from the equator to the Arctic without encountering land masses.

Thus, vortical weather systems can form in the Pacific and move northeast until they encounter the Arctic jet stream. The Arctic jet stream then forces these vortical systems to move east along the border of the Arctic air mass.

If the southward movement of the sun's ecliptic plane has allowed the jet stream to move south into the U.S., the vortical weather system will move into the U.S. in a southeast direction, unique among the various weather patterns.

Vortical weather systems that organize themselves over the U.S. will move from southwest to northeast.

Vortical weather systems that organize themselves in the Atlantic Ocean southeast of the U.S. will move in a northwest direction until they make land fall, at which point they will behave like vortical systems that form over land, and move from southwest to northeast.

Weather systems that organize themselves to the west of descending, high pressure air masses will move from west to east across the U.S.

The source of the weather that goes into these systems can be either the northward moving air masses, the vortical systems entering the U.S. in the Pacific northwest and breaking up against the western side of a descending, high pressure air mass, or a combination of both.

We currently think of the vortical weather systems as cyclones organizing themselves around low air pressure areas.

Fronts, which are the dividing line between descending high pressure air masses and established weather systems generally move from west to east unless the weather system being challenged is a vortical system, in which case the front will move from southwest to northeast.

What we are really seeing happening is northward moving weather systems encroaching on the southward moving high pressure air masses, which are challenging the encroachment.

It is a battle between decelerating air masses with high velocity and the high pressure, and therefore more stable, descending air masses!

To encroach, the northward moving air systems have to be composed of clouds and the clouds have to have some way of intermingling with the southward moving high pressure air masses.

Why do the northward moving cloud filled air masses have to intermingle with the southward moving high pressure air masses to produce weather systems?

The clouds are created by hydrogen and oxygen nuclei forming structures as a result of their potential differences with their environment. They are moving in a polar direction from the equator as a result of the pressure gradient force of the descending high pressure air masses.

The oxygen and hydrogen nuclei frozen into the ice flecks that are the clouds have the potential of being rain if they can obtain a source of electrons, heat, that will allow them to form into water molecules.

We have seen that when we move two nuclei together, we force the potential differences of the nuclei to replace orbiting electrons, and create heat.

On the other hand, when gas expands, the opposite of the compression process, it absorbs heat.

Or at least it can!

Absorbing heat means that the atoms are taking electrons out of the environment and putting them to use in their orbital clouds.

Why would they do this?

Because as the area for the atoms to expand into increases, the atoms expand into that area, and the nuclei move apart.

This can be seen by the reduction in the field, temperature, that is required to boil water the higher the water is above sea level. If we move an open pot of water from sea level to five hundred and fifty feet above sea level, the boiling point goes down one degree Fahrenheit.

The nuclei in the water molecules have moved apart as a result of the reduction in pressure associated with the increased area available for the atmosphere to occupy. This results in a reduction in the level of field replacement required to break the water down into its constituent atoms of oxygen and hydrogen.

When the nuclei move apart, the degree to which they cease to satisfy each other's potential differences increases.

This increases the potential difference in the nuclei which they attempt to satisfy by attracting electrons from the ambient field.

Decompressing gas cools because it takes heat, electrons, out of the environment.

Expanding gases artificially on the surface of the Earth is all fine and good because when the nuclei move apart, there are plenty of ambient electrons in the environment to allow them to expand with ease.

However, when the hydrogen and oxygen atoms, as well as the nitrogen atoms are rising, there is a finite number of electrons in the ambient field!

As a result, as the atoms rise, the number of electrons in the ambient field decreases.

At the same time the number of ambient electrons in the ambient field is decreasing, then, the potential differences of the nuclei of the rising atoms with the surrounding environment are increasing.

The result is the substance of the clouds and the substance of the clouds is not the substance of ice!

Ice forms out of water molecules as a result of electrons being removed from the orbiting clouds holding the atoms together in a state of dynamic equilibrium.

As the orbital clouds lose electrons, the ice forms into a physical structure with crystalline borders.

The hydrogen and oxygen nuclei that form the ice flecks that make up clouds are nuclei that have already lost their orbital clouds.

These ice flecks form as a result of the direct attraction between potential differences of the oxygen and hydrogen nuclei.

Ice forms from a water molecule whereas the ice flecks that make up the clouds are not formed from a water molecule, but directly from nuclei of the hydrogen and oxygen atoms coming together as a result of their potential differences.

Both ice and the ice flecks that make up the clouds reform into water molecules.

Icebergs drift toward the warmer waters of the equator. Ice cubes cool mint juleps.

The ice flecks have the potential of reforming into water molecules!

As they do so, they produce weather.

The problem is, the clouds are embedded in the winds that are moving northward.

These winds are in the upper atmosphere where there are no ambient electrons, there is no heat, to convert the ice flecks into water.

Even the sun's rays are no help. They are liable to rob the ice flecks of what few electrons they have available in their orbital clouds for use in establishing inductive flows.

The southward moving air masses, on the other hand, are close to the ground.

The ground alternately gives up electrons to the

atmosphere during the day and takes them back in at night.

We have already seen that it is a lot easier for the ground to give the electrons up into the atmosphere than it is for the ground to take them back at night.

Thus, the evenings provide plenty of ambient electrons to warm the cold air masses as they move south.

But the southward moving air masses, with plenty of ambient electrons, are a long way from the northward moving air masses, with their electron poor ice fleck cloud banks.

How do these clouds get at the electrons so that they can turn the ice flecks into the rain that fruits the plains?

To answer this question we have to go back and create a picture of how these two air masses move with respect to the surface of the planet.

The southward moving air masses start at the poles. Theoretically, air masses at the pole have no forward motion. However, the Arctic areas into which the northward moving air masses end their journey, lose their final ice flecks in snow and begin their southward journey encompass the Arctic circle.

As a result, the southward moving air masses will begin their journey with some motion, two to three hundred miles per hour, in an eastward direction.

However, these air masses will still have to speed up to a thousand miles per hour by the time they reach the equator.

As the southward moving, high pressure air masses move south, they are constantly speeding up.

However, they will never be moving as fast as the point on the planet over which they are moving.

As a result, if a person were standing on that point and facing in the direction toward which the air was speeding up, she would still feel a breeze on her face.

Wind to the stationary observer would appear to be blowing from the east rather than speeding up to the east.

We have to keep this picture in mind.

From the perspective of a person on the surface of the Earth, the southward moving air masses appear to be moving towards the west!

The situation is reversed with respect to the northward moving air masses. These air masses start their journey traveling at one thousand miles per hour and have to slow down to several hundred miles per hour by the time they get to the area of the Arctic circle.

There are, however, several significant differences. The northward moving air masses are moving over the southward moving air masses so that there is no geographical friction involved in the slowing process. Second, the northward moving air masses have vast expanses of ice flecks, clouds, embedded in them.

The cloud embedded portions of air masses move

differently than clear air masses.

Heavier atoms will move to the bottom of air masses that are motionless with respect to the surface of the Earth.

Heavier atoms within air masses will slow down less readily in a decelerating air mass because the heavier atoms have more momentum.

This effect, however, applies only to the atoms of the affected air masses. The cloud embedded air masses are heavier than the non cloud embedded air masses, and thus will move to the bottom of the non cloud embedded air masses.

The clouds, therefore, move to the bottom of the northward moving air masses, and it is here that the northward moving air masses have their speed in the eastward direction slowed.

Thus, as the northward moving air masses move north, they start their journey traveling east at about one thousand miles per hour.

As each point on the planet north of the point to its south is traveling slower than the point to its south, the northward moving air masses are always moving east at a greater speed than the point on the planet directly beneath them.

Thus, if a person could stand on a platform that was taller than the top of the southward moving air masses facing east, the direction the northward air masses were moving, she would feel a breeze on the back of her neck even though the northward moving air masses were slowing down as they were moving east!

In addition, if the platform was in the clouds, the breeze would be less than if the platform were above the clouds!

So, if we keep the picture we are building clear, we can make a number of statements with respect to a person standing, say, in Washington D.C.

That person is standing on the planet's surface which is moving at around eight hundred miles per hour. The person's perception, however, is one of motionlessness. She is stationary with respect to the environment that is important to her, the ground on which she is standing. The wind can be blowing from any direction, but to her perception, its speed is in relation to her stationary position.

The air around her, however, is actually accelerating in an eastward direction. However, it has not accelerated to the speed she is moving by standing on the surface of the Earth.

Thus, if there were an absence of weather systems, she would feel a steady breeze which, because it was moving to the west, would be blowing on her face.

Even though the air is accelerating, she is moving in the direction of the acceleration faster than the air is moving!

A thousand feet above her head, the air is decelerating.

However, it is still moving faster than she is moving so that if she had a thousand foot finger, she would be able to test the breeze, which would be coming from the west.

The southward moving air is always traveling slower than the surface of the Earth over which it is traveling, while the air moving north is always traveling faster than the surface of the Earth.

Our picture from Washington D.C. is idealistic in order to make it clear.

The fact is that by the time the northward moving air reaches Washington D.C., it has already formed into the weather systems that will slice into the descending high pressure air masses.

The idealistic picture of two air masses moving two different directions, while at the same time accelerating and decelerating in a third direction and with respect to a point over which they are passing is obviously not going to exist for too long a period of time.

Especially when the upper air mass has its lower portion embedded with cloud banks.

It is not hard to see what the result will be. If we stand at the equator looking north, we would see clockwise swirls of air create convection currents that cause the clouds to organize themselves into the weather systems that we see moving across the U.S.!

If we pretend we are at the north pole, we can point our right thumb toward our nose and see in what direction these convection currents would flow.

If we straighten our fingers out, our fingers will be pointing east in the direction of the Earth's rotation.

This is the direction that the two air masses are moving as they accelerate or decelerate.

The fingers themselves could represent the clouds, with the space above the finger clouds the clear upper air that collects in jet streams at various points in its northward journey. These levels are decelerating, but are moving faster than a stationary point beneath them.

The space below the finger clouds could be the clear, high pressure, southward moving air which, while it is accelerating, is moving slower with respect to the same point beneath it.

As the clouds move against the slower moving air mass beneath them, they are going to be forced down into that air mass!

If you curl your finger clouds into the lower air mass, you can picture the counterclockwise motion of these convection currents.

Of course, if we were looking at the convection currents from the equator, they would be moving in a clockwise direction.

The result of these convection currents is predictable only in its gross effect.

Obviously, as the clouds of ice flecks are sucked into

the lower air mass, they will absorb electrons from what is a warmer air mass.

We have to remember that the lower air mass warms up as it moves south but that the upper air mass is not warm and moist as popular thought pictures it.

It is not warm, moisture filled air wafting up from the equator!

The northward moving air mass lost its heat, electrons, as a product of its being forced up into an area of greater volume.

The increased potential differences of the nuclei immobilized the electrons in the ambient field, and then themselves, as they clumped together in ice flecks to satisfy each other's potential differences.

Having lunch sitting on the wing of a Boeing 777 flying south through these clouds would be a cold lunch indeed!

Weather, therefore, is created as these clouds move down into the lower air masses.

The amount of weather depends on the electrons available in the lower air masses, which is, in turn, a function of the clouds themselves, and the sunlight that they allow to reach the Earth's surface, as well as what's on that surface, water or land.

As much as we want to organize our concepts of the weather around vortical weather systems and front like configurations, these are only the gross aspects of defined weather. Its regular face is a jumble of cloud systems and storms that exist when the conditions exist that permit whatever ingredients are available to organize into the weather.

As a gross weather system, however, the convection currents created by the intermingling of the northward moving air masses with the southward moving air masses create the basic weather systems that produce the fronts and vortical systems.

To the extent that the cloud banks survive that intermingling, north/south convection systems are created that move northeast in what could be described as waves.

These weather systems travel northeast because they are organized by the northward moving air masses which have more velocity and momentum than the southward moving air mass, and east because the Earth is moving west beneath them.

These weather systems move in waves for a simple mechanical reason.

Put your two thumbs toward your nose and curl the fingers. If the fingers of your right hand represent the direction of the convection currents, then the only convection currents that could form contiguously would be ones that flow in the direction of the fingers of the left hand.

This does not occur in nature because the planet does not move from east to west.

As a result, convectional weather systems could only

form with a degree of separation in order to avoid interfering with one another.

As these convectional weather systems move north, they are slicing into the southward moving, high pressure air masses.

These southward moving air masses began their journey at the pole, and are both cold and dry in the sense that they lack hydrogen and oxygen molecules.

They did not become cold as a result of giving up motion to the environment and they did not become dry as a result of air pressure squeezing the water out of the air!

These air masses are cold and dry because they lack electrons.

They lack electrons because the north pole is out of the direct line of the sun's rays.

The sun's rays not only liberate electrons on the surface of the Earth, they break down in the atmosphere and on the surface of the Earth, adding electrons to the environment.

As the air masses move north past the Arctic circle, the electrons in the environment become increasingly less, and the environment removes electrons from the atoms and molecules that make up the air.

The oxygen and hydrogen nuclei move together as a result, precipitating as snow.

The remaining nuclei move closer together because of

their potential differences and this creates the weight that produces the air pressure that causes the air mass to move south into the less dense, warmer air masses.

As these dry, cold air masses move south, they take in electrons, the nuclei of the atoms move further apart, and the air masses produce less pressure.

A vortical storm system develops as a convectional weather system moves north along the east side of a descending air mass.

If we pick two points on the equator, and draw a line from each point to the north pole, we will have a triangle with which we can visualize how vortical weather systems form.

The triangle will have an east edge. This east edge is the edge toward which the air in the descending air mass is accelerating.

Air at the top of the triangle is not moving east while air at the base is moving east at about a thousand miles an hour.

The westward moving winds of a northward moving convectional system would find less eastward resistance the further north they were in the convectional system.

To visualize how the northward moving convectional systems move, we can draw a line from the east point on the base of the triangle parallel with the west line of the triangle.

If you put the heels of your hands together and spread

the fingers and palms outward, we can see the dual effect.

The left had represents the southward moving air mass speeding up the further toward the palm it is.

The right hand represents the northward moving convectional system which is slowing down as it moves north.

If the convectional system is embedded with clouds and the southward moving air mass has an excess of electrons, then as the clouds are drawn down into the southward moving air mass, the oxygen and hydrogen atoms are going to turn into water molecules.

As the clouds turn into water, the water slows. Remember that the air mass in which the clouds are embedded is slowing, the clouds slowing more than the air itself, and as the clouds turn to water, they slow at an increasing rate.

If you return to the space between the heels of your palms, the clouds in the northward moving convectional systems slow into the space between the fingers as they turn into water molecules.

If there is sufficient weather, the northern end of the northward moving convectional system slows into the north side of the southward moving air mass, reaches a point of resistance and begins to spread south, curving in a counterclockwise direction until the eastward moving air mass takes over and pushes it east.

Thus, the convectional weather system's motion north

is turned into a vortical motion in a counterclockwise direction!

The more clouds the northward moving convectional system has and the more electrons the southward moving air mass has, the greater the vortical system becomes, the more defined the vortical pattern, and the more weather it produces.

The weather producing system, with its atoms moving apart as they form into water molecules as the system moves into the high pressure area, creates the air pressure differential, the dropping barometer, that characterizes an approaching storm.

Because the storm has become vortical, its winds do not move it, but rather it moves as a result of its friction with the land over which its clouds are being converted to water molecules.

The greater the process of cloud conversion to water molecules, the greater the pressure differential and the bigger the storm.

The greatest differential between these vortical air systems is found in the Atlantic ocean southeast of the U.S.

The sun's ecliptic plane is the point on the Earth at which the sun is directly overhead.

As the sun's ecliptic plane starts south, at the summer solstice, approaching the autumnal equinox, the high pressure southward moving air masses begin to pick up the vast numbers of electrons generated by the North

American summer.

At the same time, the sun's rays are breaking down vast amounts of water molecules at the equator to form clouds.

These clouds, embedded in the northward moving convectional systems mix with the electron filled southward moving air mass to produce the giant vortical storms called hurricanes!

Hurricanes actually move in a northeast direction. However, because they are moving northeast slower than the Earth under them is rotating, they are moving northwest with respect to the east coast of North America.

The ocean beneath the hurricane is providing little friction to maintain its speed. As the winds that make it up slow down faster the further north they sweep, the storm follows in a northwest direction so long as the northern winds are not blocked by a descending high pressure air mass.

When the hurricane makes land fall, friction increases and it tacks northeast, which is the same with vortical systems formed over land.

As convectional weather systems move north, the area available for them to occupy becomes less.

They can push their way up between ridges in the descending high pressure air masses to form fronts.

Fronts are the dividing line between the high pressure, descending air masses and the northward moving convectional systems characterized by weather bearing clouds.

The western side of a descending air mass may be strong enough to block the movement east of a northward moving convectional system.

The block will remain until the northward moving system collects enough weather to encroach on the southward moving air mass.

The process of moving fronts involves the friction of the high pressure air mass rotating with the Earth against the eastward pressure of the northward moving convectional system which, while slowing down, is still moving faster than the points on the Earth over which it is traveling.

Vortical systems moving southeast from the Pacific northwest can also create these encroachments and the resulting fronts.

Northward moving vortical systems can directly challenge southward moving air masses to create horizontal fronts.

And finally, northward moving convectional systems that fail to establish vortical systems to the east of the descending air mass collect on the east side of the air mass and move northeast.

When I had the discussion about what makes the wind blow some forty years ago, I had been dead wrong about why the air was blowing in from the northwest.

On the other hand, so had everybody else!

I have to admit that when I started this book, I had no idea why the wind was blowing from the northwest.

I still don't.

It could have been the result of several situations.

However, it wasn't blowing from high pressure to low pressure, and it wasn't blowing because of the Coriolis effect.

It was blowing because it was slowing down.

It had to be then.

And it has to be now!

10   The Forecast

What is the forecast?

My guess is as good as yours!

Well, not quite.

Probably not even close, because I don't follow the weather.

If I did, I would follow the weather where I live, and not anywhere else.

And that's the only way that you can attempt to predict the weather.

Seems a contradiction, doesn't it?

You have to follow to predict!

To understand what appears to be a paradox, one of those beloved contradictions that validate the most harebrained theories consensual science can propose, we can look at Washington D.C.'s subway system.

Washington has an excellent subway system with some very deep stations. These stations are served by some very long elevators.

These elevators move at a steady speed up tubes with curved concrete walls having periodic seams dividing the wall's poured concrete sections.

If the elevator were really long, long enough for the

ride to span generations, we could live and die without ever knowing any environment other than the seams periodically passing on the wall.

After awhile, we might conclude that the seams weren't passing us, but rather we were moving, passing the seams.

If we were to invent a watch, we could measure the time it takes to pass each seam, and even measure lives by the number of seams.

We could find out that each seam was twenty legs long!

We could then dazzle our children with our ability to predict when the next seam would pass, concocting some sort of razzmatazz about all matter moving in a straight line as long as the seams didn't alter its motion.

It wouldn't matter what we said because experience has told us that the seams are going to pass on a regular basis, and known or unbeknownst to us will continue to do so for as long as the conditions that are creating the physical relationship that causes them to pass continue to exist.

There is no forecast.

There is no prediction.

There is no cause and effect.

There are just physical consequences given a specific set of physical conditions.

We don't have to know the conditions.   On the escalator, like on the Earth, we could be totally ignorant of what is causing the motion and still know that the next seam was going to come at a specific time.

With respect to the weather, however, there are no continuing physical relationships.

Without continuing physical relationships, there are no chances of fooling ourselves into making predictions, forecasts, soothsaying to the inattentive.

It is the continuing physical relationship of the solar system that deludes astronomers into claiming the ability to predict the position of the planets using Newtonian mechanics and its associated mathematical systems.

The sun, it is said, is traveling through space at some half million miles per hour, dragging the planets along behind in their elliptical orbits as it does.

At the end of each day, the planets are millions of miles from wherever they were that morning!

We don't know where they are to start with, other than maybe in the arm of a spiral galaxy, we don't know where they're going, and we don't know where they're going to be when they get there.

So, no one can predict where the planets are, let alone where they'll be.

Well, maybe not, the gurus of science say, but we can damn sight predict where the planets will be with respect to one another. They were all put in motion five billion, four hundred million, six hundred and nineteen thousand, five hundred sixty three years and fifty five days ago, give or take a day or two, and they have been in the exact same courses ever since.

All we have to do is measure those courses, and we will be able to measure back and forward the ten billion, six hundred million, etc. years they have left to determine exactly where they have been and will be in relation to one another.

Hmmm.

We don't even know where the moon will be tomorrow, let alone how fast the Earth will be rotating!

And, to really put the foot to it, we haven't any way at all to determine what the speed of the Earth is in its orbit because the only way we can determine speed is by reference to the motion of other bodies in the solar system.

The motion of these bodies, driven by the rate of the sun's combustion process, changes uniformly so that there is no baseline to measure changes in that motion.

We can't tell if anything is speeding up or slowing down because all points of reference are speeding up and slowing down proportionately!

So what are these marvelous Newtonian Mechanics that are doing all this powerful predicting?

If, in reality, we can't predict where anything is going to be tomorrow, how can we claim that Newtonian Mechanics predicts anything?

Newtonian Mechanics supposedly proved that the planets moved in accordance with the inverse square law of gravity. If gravity diminished inversely with the square of the distance from its source, then the momentum of the matter would precisely counteract the inverse square law.

We have seen that the amount of matter, the number of nuclei per area, determines momentum, so how do we determine how much matter is in the moon or a planet to determine its momentum?

After all, even if we go there, we can't crack the moon or a planet open and determine what's inside.

Newton solved this insoluble problem by using size!

He said the moon is such and such a volume, the Earth is such and such a volume, and we can calculate the units of matter per volume to come up with momentum.

As the momentum exactly matched the inverse square law, the inverse square law controlled the movement of the planets.

Huh?

Gravity is a direct force between bodies.

How can it control movement?

Well, maybe not movement, but...

And besides, Newton was wrong about the units of matter. The moon is too big for the inverse square law which meant that it must be made out of Swiss cheese, or it is hollow, or its back side is caved in.

How can you accept a law as fact under the rules of the scientific method if the verification doesn't work?

"That," the gurus reply, "is just what we were getting at. We don't have to prove something that is proved repeatedly. We can predict where the planets will be exactly. Just because Newton didn't understand the concept of mass..."

"Mass? What's mass?" reply we inattentive dolts.

"The amount of units of matter per volume, of course. That's what the inverse square law predicts."

"Wait a minute." We pause, scratching our collective heads. "Let's see if we can get this straight. Newton set out to prove the inverse square law using size to determine the amount of matter in a planet in order to calculate its momentum.

"When it was discovered that the use of size to determine the amount of matter in a planet never agreed with an inverse square law, you geniuses didn't throw out the law, you used it to determine how much matter was in a planet?

"Let's restate that because we can't be right." This isn't easy to say because our jaw is bouncing off our shoes.

"When the facts disproved Newton's hypothesis that there was an inverse square law associated with the movement of the planets, you just made up matter to make the non law work?"

"We didn't make up matter. We discovered that by

using the inverse square law, we could determine the existence of matter.

"We can tell you exactly what is in the center of the planet Jupiter. Without the inverse square law, by golly, we wouldn't know that fact!"

"But," we cry, "you can't independently verify what is in the center of Jupiter!

"You've made up a law which can't be proved, and then used it to create matter you can't prove exists!"

"We don't have to prove it exists," the gurus reply, "because we have discovered the inverse square law, and it dictates what is in the center of Jupiter. No independent verification is necessary."

"We thought the scientific method involved making testable predictions."

"Scientific fact never has to be tested!"

Basically, what we have with mass/gravity and the inverse square law is the bald assumption that God put the planets in motion some time in the past. God also created a force which is a property of matter. That force exactly counteracts the force God used to put the planets in motion.

And golly, that's the way things are. It's like the Earth is round. It's a fact!

In reality, however, if we want to know where the planets are going to be tomorrow, we are going to have to know where they were yesterday.

We can predict that the moon is going to come up a certain way because it always comes up in that way. The sun comes up in the morning because it has always come up in the morning.

The fact that it is never exactly the same, that we always have to make adjustments, is just something we do as a matter of course to correct prior errors.

What about the marvelous ability to send rockets to Jupiter and beyond? After all, consensual science uses this technological accomplishment as continuing proof of mass/gravity's powers of prediction.

Navigational teams meet incessantly for orbit determination, which in laymen's terms means to find out where the hell the rocket is, and then figure out where the hell to send it if they succeed in finding out where it is.

For those wishing to delve into the technical basis for this highly complex area, after using the time lapse of radio signals to determine distance, and a doppler shift to estimate speed, the navigational team keeps clicking pictures in the hopes of triangulating the rocket's location.

It has nothing to do with predicting other than to illustrate the fact that false claims about successful predictions are made not only to prove a theory, but to maintain the belief, actually the self delusion as to the theory's factual nature.

To listen to the gurus, many of whom have never

applied nut to bolt, science is not only responsible for technology, it is technology!

Newtonian Mechanics and the Coriolis effect have two things in common: They each have an obsession with rockets and they are both bull crap explanations dressed up in mathematical mysticism to explain something we can already measure, in the case of planetary movement, by putting a stick in the ground to sight the sun's motion in relation to the Earth, and in the case of wind, by putting a flag on the stick!

They are metaphors for mindlessness!

No navigator ever waited on Newton or Coriolis to speed the safe delivery of his valued cargo.

I have a theory about the obsession of using mathematics to explain physical phenomena. When you can't think, count.

Mathematics are absolutely necessary for verifying the facts that exist in physical reality. If we want to know how objects fall, we can't sit back in a room somewhere and say how they fall, we have to go out and measure how they fall. If we want to know which way the wind blows, we have to stick our finger up in the air.

If we want to create a consistent picture of physical phenomena, then we have to know the boundaries of the physical world.

The only way we can do that is to create a way to compare the hard edges of reality, and the events those hard edges are involved in, each with the others.

To do this, we have to create tools of the mind, agreed upon measuring units which we can hold against reality, and in doing so define that reality.

But once we know the reality, we cannot use the mathematical systems we devised to measure reality to explain that reality for us.

Mathematicians deal with equations and equations require terms. Because the world contains an infinite number of terms, and equations can only hold a finite number of terms, the mathematical process has to limit the portion of reality to the number of terms it can handle in its equations.

With respect to the movement of the planets around the sun, mathematics removes the cause of motion from the equations because it is one term too many!

We have no more idea what is making the planets move than we had two thousand years ago.

Probably less, because two thousand years ago Aristotle at least attempted to explain motion on a mechanical basis, whereas our rational minds just abdicate movement to God, or God's minion, conservation, where motion is in a closed system, whatever that is.

How can we expect to explain anything when we can't even explain why the planet on which we sit is moving around the sun?

Using the Coriolis effect to explain the winds is not

much better. When we can't make it work out, we are in the same boat that Newtonian proponents are in when they can't make size work for the inverse square law.

When something doesn't work, we can't just abandon it, we have to make it better. Thus, we mathematise the Coriolis effect with the isobaric differentials created by the pressure-gradient force until, like creators of the green cheese moon, we torture something into existence that approximates reality.

And that's all we need, something to approximate reality, a hocus pocus set of mumbo jumbo that we can point to in order to claim that our predictions are not sourced on a pointy hat covered with stars and half moons but are in fact based on an analytical consideration of all the reason and solid factual consideration that society requires of its soothsayers.

Even if it is so much jiggery-pokery!

We can't predict the future, and that's a fact.

And if we do make a prediction that turns out to be correct, the scientific prediction that proves the testable hypothesis, we haven't proven anything.

But, we believe we now understand something that we don't!

By analogizing the wind to a rocket, we think that we have found the answer to what makes the wind blow.

What happens when we think we have found the answer to a question?

We don't ask any more questions!

When we find that the rocket idea doesn't work, we graft some more fins on the rocket and send it up for a second try.

This process is universal in the consensual science of today, which uses reputation as its authority.

If we are looking at the weather, and we find that air pressure increases and decreases, then we decide that the reason it is increasing and decreasing is that there is more air or less air.

As air pressure is determined by how tall an air column is, then if there is greater air pressure, then there must be a taller column of air.

But when this doesn't wash, we say, well, the air is more dense. That's a function of atoms, so let's go over and see what the experts say.

By limiting ourselves to only bits and pieces of the overall picture, we have abdicated interrelated elements of the picture to other people who are also only looking at bits and pieces of the picture.

Instead of building knowledge, the elevation of mathematics to the status of truth giver has fragmented knowledge to the point where knowledge is incomprehensible.

So, when we go over to the atom squishing truth givers, they say, well, that's simple, when you compress atoms, their nuclei move closer together.

But that's the question!

As a result, you walk around scratching your head saying that the pressure increases because the atoms move closer together as a result of their being under greater pressure.

Gee, something about that doesn't sound right. Maybe if you turn it around, and say that greater pressure compresses atoms which result in greater pressure...

And all the time you're walking around scratching your head, your not lifting up your head and looking at the real world around you, looking at it with your eyes instead of your recall, seeing what is there instead of seeing what you have been told is there.

It's fortunate that it is just a matter of years before we can compress all knowledge into an equation that will fit on a postage stamp.

After all, the gurus tell us that The Theory of Everything is only an undiscovered measurement away.

We will then truly be able to look at the face of God and know His or Her mind.

On the slim chance that you and I are not among the privileged ones that will be able to sit at His knee and ask Him how He makes the planets move or the wind blow, perhaps it would behoove us to get off our mental duffs, stop assuming that we know everything there is to know, and get to work coming up with a consistent picture of physical reality.

It's only hard to propose answers when you have no questions.

And when we spend our time forecasting facts that don't exist in the belief that finding those facts will verify our beliefs, then our questions will evaporate before the winds that blow through our empty minds!

The Persecution of
Mildred Dunlap

a novel

PAULETTE MAHURIN

BLUE PALM PRESS
Santa Barbara

ISBN: 978-0-9771866-1-7

Published by Blue Palm Press
PO Box 61255, Santa Barbara, CA 93160, USA

Cover: Mahurin family photo, courtesy of Terry Mahurin

Design/production by Margaret Dodd, Studio K Communication Arts
Printed in the United States of America